YOU'RE A
BEAUTIFUL
*Mess*TERPIECE

A GUIDE TO PRIORITIZING THE
God-given dream
YOU'VE BEEN ENTRUSTED
TO PURSUE & SHARE

DEANA FARRELL

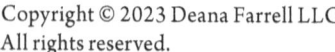

YOU'RE A BEAUTIFUL MESSTERPIECE
A guide to prioritizing the God-given dream you've been entrusted to pursue & share

ISBN: 979-8-9880599-0-5

The information in this book is for educational and inspirational purposes only. The opinions expressed in this book are those of the author and not of any affiliated organizations.

The reader assumes full responsibility for any actions taken based on the information contained in this book. The author shall have no liability or responsibility to any person or entity with the respect to any loss or damage caused or alleged to be caused directly or indirectly by the information contained in this book.

Editing by Lasting Legacies Publishing LLC
Book Design by bookery.design
Author Photo by Maverick Photo Studio

FOR WE ARE GOD'S MASTERPIECE.
HE HAS CREATED US ANEW IN

Christ Jesus,

SO WE CAN DO THE GOOD THINGS
HE PLANNED FOR US LONG AGO.

Ephesians 2:10 NLT

YOU'RE A BEAUTIFUL *Mess*TERPIECE

CONTENTS

RELATE TO YOUR GREATNESS, NOT YOUR WEAKNESS

- Unknown

INTRODUCTION

Valued, Amazing, & Loved

IF YOUR MORNING ROUTINE OF A TEN-MINUTE-OR-
LESS DEVOTIONAL, grabbing the to-go cup for breakfast, and
calling yesterday's make-up "today's smokey eye" isn't quite the
dreamy life you imagined for yourself, then you're in the right place!

Ahh, to be found living your dream life. One where your success
is measured more by your influence and impact than what you
wear, the car you drive, who you're with, or where you live. One
that allows you to own how you got there—the fumbles, stumbles,
and even the grumbles along the way, as well as what was lost and
gained. One that's full of success and significance because you
stayed focused on what mattered most more than what grabbed
your attention at the moment.

While that may be an excellent dream life, the strategic plan
needed to get there often gets lost in the mix of day-to-day reali-
ties. It can be pretty hard to get off life's hamster wheel long enough
to conduct an honest "where am I now?" evaluation. Assessing
just how much of your life is spent simply existing and surviving instead of living and thriving can be quite the challenge, and
frankly, daunting.

You're probably already keenly aware of this gap between where you want to be—living your envisioned dream life—and the one striving to thrive in the midst of your daily reality. And as you seek ways to close that gap for yourself, your inner comparison critic may be shouting, *"What am I missing? What am I doing wrong?" "What is she doing so right?"* or the worst one, *"What's wrong with me?"*

Still, you continue to pursue those badges of #hustle, #girlboss, #happy, #blessed, and titles like it, all day long. Mainly because you just don't want to give up *looking* like you're living—or at least pursuing—the dream life.

And there's the line that's blurred between looking and living. We often look at others' lives with envy and then attempt to emulate them. But why? Is that really *your* dream? Is that the pain and effort you want to commit to in order to "fake it 'til you make it?"

As Christians, and especially as women in business, we can often fall prey to the pressures of the "having it all and balancing it well" persona, which leaves us on that never-ending hamster wheel of frustration.

Part of the problem could come from envisioning the dream life as a straight-line path. (Hand raised over here 'cause that's how I tend to lay out my dream plan.) Knowing how unrealistic that is, the concession now is to at least imagine the dream plan as an easy-to-spot, yet winding (there's the realistic part) yellow brick road. But the truth is that's just not how it works. The way to your dream life doesn't follow some straight-line path or an easy-to-find, and follow, yellow brick road.

The way to your dream is just like life: *messy.* And these are the very things we'll dive into together in this book.

If you feel like I'm picking on you or making assumptions about you, relax. Know that I've been there trying all those fake it 'til you make it "looks" before, as well as taking on the actual looks from others when my life didn't measure up to their dreams and ideals *for* me. I've even attempted mapping out the "perfect road" only to find I was either on the wrong one or not yet equipped for the one in front of me. Whew, what a mess that was!

YOUR DREAM'S CPR

The heart behind this book is to help you explore, accept, and pursue not just any dream, but your God-given dream. Here you'll learn to understand and define the differences between a dream you have, one other's project on you, and the dream that has been divinely entrusted to *you*.

You'll likely come to realize all your dream really needs is some CPR—**C**ore values, **P**rioritization, and **R**esources. Within these pages, you'll find the guidance and the much-needed CPR to breathe life into that dream God entrusted you to bring to the world; the dream you've been uniquely designed, purposefully commissioned, and strategically positioned to deliver!

Here you'll be supported and encouraged to finally untangle the messes that have been holding you back and hindering your progress as it relates to your dream. Within this book, you'll discover a repeatable process that you can (and should) customize in order to define your God-given dream and align it with your day-to-day reality.

Some of this book includes my personal stories, pitfalls, and a-ha moments along the way, but more importantly, it offers practical and tactical tools to help you along *your* way. I pray this book will become a catalyst for fortifying your faith, energizing your life, and bolstering your business.

Listen, I'm by no means an expert, but I bet I've been in your shoes before. I know what it's like to be a bundle of excitement and ambition pursuing the dream one minute and a defeated, doubting ball of nerves the next. I've hesitated, confused, questioned, and definitely procrastinated on the way to understanding and pursuing my God-given dream and I don't want that to be part of your story.

As a matter of fact, I initially thought this book was supposed to be a Christian devotional for women focused on one particular biblical passage. Once I started writing, though, this book became so much more than what I first imagined. I never would have guessed it would become a book that has me sharing my personal messes, experiences, experiments, and successes all in an effort to help *you* close the gap between where you are today and where your God-given dream can take you. But that's what God does with our efforts; He turns them into more than we could imagine, if we let Him.

MAKING THE MOST OF THIS BOOK

Although there are chapters that can absolutely be stand-alone resources, skipping around may cause you to miss the necessary foundational work to gain the perspective, purpose, and push you'll need to make progress toward the real dream—the God-given one you've been entrusted with for the benefit of others.

To make it easier to see and understand "where you are in the process," the book is broken into four parts: Define, Discover, Determine, and of course, Do It! As you work through each part, you'll be able to confidently answer things like who, what, when, where, how, and why as they relate to the God-given dream you've been divinely assigned.

ASSIGNMENTS AND VALS

You're a Beautiful MESSterpiece is written with an entrepreneurial woman in mind. Specifically, one who may have forgotten what a Valued, Amazing Lady (VAL) she is while in the midst of trying to sharpen her faith, enhance her life, and grow her business! It's also a bit of the permission slip she's been looking for; the one that allows her to prove herself right by aligning with what God says, she *was* made for more! I call this entire process Prioritized Focus and it's essentially the way you keep in alignment with your assignment.

VALs are who I believe God has assigned me to guide, pray for, and share my attempts, experiments, and discoveries through speaking and writing. The more I lean into this assignment, the more I find myself in awe of the divine GPS (God's Positioning System) that keeps me right where I'm supposed to be. The same is true for you, too. It's no accident that you're here reading these pages right now.

The goal is for you to finish this book recognizing you were created to *live* your life, not just survive it. Here you'll be supported and prayerfully armed to handle whatever messes life throws your way.

VAL, if you feel like a mess or your past pieces are swirling around you like a tornado in Kansas, trust the Master to transform every messy piece into a personalized brick on your own easy-to-spot, yellow brick road. Pieces like hurt, disappointment, doubt, rejection, and all. the. things are being repurposed and laid as the foundation to something incredibly beautiful ... *you*. And it's because you are **V**alued, **A**mazing, and so very **L**oved!

DEFINE

DREAMS & DIRECTIONS:
YES, PLEASE

THE MESSES YOU'VE had, made, or led you to where you are today, cannot mess up Whose you are, and what's been prepared and planned ahead *for* you.

Here's where you may want to grab a pen to actively participate, or even some highlighters and a notebook.

YOU CAN BE
BOTH A WORK IN
PROGRESS AND A
MASTERPIECE AT
THE SAME TIME

—unknown

CHAPTER 1

No Messed Opportunities

LIFE'S MESSY.

Did you catch yourself agreeing with that statement while at the same time, your brain just *flipped it against you*? You know, as in thinking thoughts like, "Ugh! Why is my life such a mess?" or "Yep, I'm a mess," and other sentiments of subconscious self-sabotage?

If you can relate to that kind of self-talk, know you're not alone. As a matter of fact, there are some who not only entertain such self-sabotaging thoughts but go as far as to claim them as their very identity.

The reality is, life *is* messy. Not just for some, but for all of us who are part of this thing called the human race. Now, whether life's messes are accepted as an identity or merely a fact has a lot to do with your perspective, experience, and the work you put into finding out the difference.

Before I learned some very important principles, mindset shifts, and tools to help me flip that narrative, I was one of those people. I took on the role and title of being a mess instead of recognizing it as a circumstance, not an identity.

It took quite a while until I understood and accepted that yes, life is, in fact, messy … but I don't have to claim ownership of it all. In other words, I could own my perceptions and experiences as they relate to the messes *in my life*, but it didn't mean I had to own *being a mess*. Note the separation there: between identifying *as a mess* and *life's messes*. One is within my control and the other is not.

When this awareness began to take root, the question that seemingly needed immediate attention was, "When am I more of the messer-upper and when am I the mess-ee?" (You're welcome for those new vocabulary words, by the way.) As in, when am I part of what's causing the mess *in* my life (my responsibility), and when is it coming from someone/somewhere else (outside of my control)?

Looking back now, there was a time in my life that ultimately became a defining moment. I'm sure you have one, too; a defining moment from what seemed like an insurmountable mess at the time. Maybe you know what it is, or maybe the realization of it hasn't fully come together for you yet.

My defining moment came more than two decades ago during the 9-11 era. At the time, I had been married for about three years and we had a soon-to-be two-year-old daughter, and I was about fifteen weeks pregnant with our would-be second child. What I chalked up as "normal" marital issues were about to become much more amplified.

I went to my second ultrasound appointment alone. I got the news alone. And I wept alone (until my parents found out). I needed comfort, reassurance, and frankly, to feel loved at that moment, all of which I thought was just a phone call away.

As I sat in the parking lot trying to get my thoughts together, I dialed his number. I did my best to hold it together as I explained to him that apparently, the baby died somewhere around eight weeks, just two weeks after hearing the heartbeat at the first visit. I had been carrying our no longer living child for six weeks! I told him as best I understood, this is called a missed miscarriage and that surgery was now required for my health.

Let's just say that conversation was not the loving, comforting, or reassurance I had hoped to hear. Looking back, I guess in some way I recognized this tragic disappointment and hurt as a pivotal moment, but one that would bring us closer and make us stronger.

Two days later it was my mom who brought me to the hospital and gave me a hug with tears in her eyes. Watching her walk away holding my happy little toddler's hand is a moment forever etched in my mind. I never felt more alone, abandoned, lacking in partnership, and disappointed than I did at that moment.

In the months that followed, I finally stopped asking to go to counseling to help save our marriage. By now I was trying to just live "normally" and do things like taking my daughter to the park or to the library for toddler groups. The maybe not-so-normal part would be that while we were at the library, I would seek out books related to helping me rescue my marriage. At this point, I thought it was my only hope. I needed a lifeline of some sort, and I was too embarrassed and defeated to talk to anyone. At checkout, I would mix the books with my daughter's selections to read at home while she was napping and he was at work. Then I'd hide them between the mattress and the box spring so he wouldn't know that I was not in agreement that "our marriage was just fine."

I was desperate to fix whatever "it" was that was wrong with me. As that was the narrative that I was hearing and supported now by what was swirling around in my head. I thought, "it must be me," and "why can't I accept that this marriage is 'good enough?'" deep down I knew there was something wrong, but couldn't seem to separate it from it being me. "Putting on a happy face" became my modus operandi as I tried my best to not let my "I'm such a mess" show.

Turns out I wasn't hiding my mess so well. A few years and another daughter later, I went to confide to my dad that I was finally going to leave and get a divorce. Standing there waiting for the disappointment, the you betters, you should haves, and you're going tos … I was stunned at what I actually heard. I'll never forget his words: "It's about time," followed by, "what do you need?" Relief, support, hope, and loving reassurance were all wrapped in his words that day.

It still took several months between the time I made the decision and actually started the process. Maybe it was because I knew in some way, I was trading one kind of mess for another. Oh, and it got a lot messier, but at least I no longer saw myself *as* the mess, just the mess I was no longer willing to be *in*. That separation of me being the mess, and the messy situation, helped me begin to thrive.

Remember I said earlier how I thought I was doing a good job at hiding "I'm such a mess" in my day-to-day living? Now people were saying things to me like, "Welcome back, Deana" or "Wow, it's like you woke up from a coma or something." My demeanor was different, my outlook was different, and even my clothes got brighter! Sheesh! How much of that mess did I allow to become my perspective and sadly, my very identity? Apparently, quite a bit.

Please, don't think this example of my defining moment leading to my divorce is an easy answer or your permission slip out of a messy marriage. This was sharing a defining moment with you and how I responded. And don't think this was the only messy thing I've navigated, puh-shaw! There have been a *lot* more hurts, heartaches, and devastations before this, and definitely since. In some, I was the messer-upper (had responsibility), and in others the mess-ee (the recipient). I've had to deal with and try to understand messes like rejection, mental illness, gossip, unforgiveness, betrayal, accusations, crippling grief … need I go on? Yes, there's more, as I'm sure is the case for you, too. I'm not trying to impress you with my messes, nor am I assuming yours "aren't as bad" as mine. That's something we both deal with, isn't it? People trying to discount our mess to shine their mess badge brighter (eye-roll). And for what? To make you feel worse?

For me, in the midst of many of those circumstances and situations, there were times when I told myself that my life was a mess, and everything was pointing to *me*—*just one big mess!* I also believed that everyone could see "it" on me like it was my nametag. Ugh! Looking back, so much of my day-to-day living was stolen because of those beliefs.

Living. Did you catch that part? Believing your life is a mess—or worse, that *you're* a mess—is stealing your focus from actual living.

When was the last time your own beliefs were at the root of why you were merely existing and just surviving? You were meant to have life and to live it fully. On purpose for purpose.

Whatever "this mess" is for you right now, it does not define you, but it certainly has the potential to refine you.

The point I'm trying to make here is that you have the opportunity to decide if your messy moments become defining, refining, or both.

You have the opportunity to decide if your messy moments become defining, refining, or both.

THE THIEF COMES
ONLY TO STEAL
AND KILL AND
DESTROY; I HAVE
COME THAT THEY
MAY HAVE LIFE,
AND HAVE IT TO
THE FULL.

– John 10:10 NIV

VAL, (that's you, remember, Valued, Amazing Lady) we are about to embark on a journey together that will help you define your own perceptions and experiences as they relate to you and the messes *in* your life. Note the separation there: between you and *life's messes.* The goal is for you to finish this book recognizing how much living and thriving you can do (and how you were made to do it) no matter what mess gets thrown your way!

DON'T MISS YOUR DREAM

In our relentless pursuit and perception of *the dream*, we often miss something. It's a big issue that needs to be addressed, which is: You must understand who you need to become in order to handle your dream.

Your dream—the one entrusted *to you.* Don't miss that little part, the one that will make all the difference. There's a big difference between chasing/pursuing the dream (a generic one) and your dream (the one specific to and for you).

When you fail to address this difference, you end up sacrificing what really matters in the end for what you want (or what others want for you) at the moment. And for many, that's trading a life of purpose and a meaningful legacy for a short-lived knockoff of someone else's dreamy, Insta-worthy-looking life.

Don't be her.

Don't be the one who is exhausting herself, wasting energy only to look like she's living the dream. That same energy could instead be used to build *her* dream, the one specific to and for her. But first, she needs to become the person who can handle it!

How about you? Do you want to just be someone who merely looks like you're living the dream (generic) or the person who can handle your dream (the one that is specific only to you)?

I believe that your dream is the vision God shared *with you* for the purpose of others finding Him *through you*. He has specifically gifted, equipped, and prepared you for how you were meant to make a difference in this world. And that difference can only be accomplished through your understanding and alignment with your God-given dream.

There is a verse that I believe supports this idea. My hope is that you'll ponder and internalize it for yourself:

FOR WE ARE HIS WORKMANSHIP, CREATED IN CHRIST JESUS FOR GOOD WORKS, WHICH GOD PREPARED BEFOREHAND THAT WE SHOULD WALK IN THEM.

- Ephesians 2:10 NKJV

Take note of the word, "workmanship" and consider its meaning. Its Greek origin is *poiēma* and means a work that has been made ahead of time, which the verse reiterates. When pronounced, *poiēma* sounds a lot like our English word, "poem." I love the definition of a poem from *The American Heritage Dictionary*: "A verbal composition designed to convey experiences, ideas, or emotions in a vivid and imaginative way, characterized by the use of language chosen for its sound and suggestive power." And just for added measure, some biblical translations use the word "workmanship" as a *masterpiece*.

All of this means you can step into your God-given dream knowing that it's been prepared *for* you ... and that you get to show up as God's workmanship, poem, or masterpiece. Take your pick!

That specific *for you* dream is the seed God planted in your heart. Once you recognize it for what it is, your job is to make sure it grows and bears fruit.

Here's a little side lesson on fruit: A fruit's purpose is to protect the seed until it is mature enough to be shared. Once the fruit is ripe (mature) its goal is twofold: 1) spread its seeds as far and wide as possible, and 2) support and nourish the other fruit. How's that for a visualization of how important and needed your dream is for you ... and others?

Think of all the ways we can grow and mature in love, joy, peace, perseverance, gentleness, goodness, faith, humility, and self-control. I love how verses 22-23 in Galatians 5 points out that no one is against those! A life focused on spreading those things far and wide for the benefit of others is the very definition of mature fruits. And God has given each of us the ability to pursue fruitful maturity with passion through our dreams.

BUT THE FRUIT OF THE SPIRIT IS LOVE, JOY, PEACE, LONGSUFFERING, GENTLENESS, GOODNESS, FAITH, MEEKNESS, TEMPERANCE: AGAINST SUCH, THERE IS NO LAW.

— Galatians 5:22-23 KJV

My prayer for you is that you'll come to understand your God-given dream and be willing to put in the work required to protect, grow, and share it. Those tasks and what they will require of you won't always be easy, but I can tell you it's not going to be work that you dread. That's encouraging, right?

Know that this work will stretch you, but also strengthen you beyond your imagination. It will bring people and opportunities that consistently knock your socks off. You'll experience deeper fulfillment than your biggest empty space.

There is no empty space in you that God doesn't already know about and have a plan, strategy, and process for in order to make you whole.

But you won't experience such fulfillment beyond your biggest empty space if you keep ignoring His calls, or trying to fill those voids with other things or people! You see, once you accept your dream as being God-given, the work becomes an exciting adventure. You begin to look forward to discovering what's on the next page because you realize that it was written just for you.

From here on out VAL—yes, that's you remember, *V*alued, *A*mazing *L*ady—we're going to put in the work to show that you're ready to impact this world through that cRaZy, BIG, God-given dream of yours!

And, for the record, I'm working to become the person I need to be in order to handle my cRaZy, BIG, God-given dream right there with ya! Let's prove there are no messed opportunities, just better and more accurate perceptions about them.

YET GOD HAS
MADE EVERYTHING
BEAUTIFUL FOR ITS
OWN TIME. HE HAS
PLANTED ETERNITY
IN THE HUMAN HEART,
BUT EVEN SO, PEOPLE
CANNOT SEE THE
WHOLE SCOPE OF
GOD'S WORK FROM
BEGINNING TO END.

– Ecclesiastes 3:11 NLT

CHAPTER 2

Right on Time

IT CAN BE A ROLLER-COASTER OF A RIDE, UNTAN-
GLING WHAT YOU'VE BEEN TOLD ABOUT YOUR DREAM.
Maybe you've heard it's too big, unrealistic, impossible, or that
you're too old, young, late, soon .... Those can become seeds of
doubt and if left to grow, they can really get you messed up in your
feelings and wanting to give up on your dream!

It's no wonder you may be feeling broken, busted, and disgusted
on the ride to your dream so far. I see you nodding your head in
agreement, curling the corner of your lip with a little "um-hmm"
under your breath. Is it obvious I've been on this ride before?

I hate to break it to you, but this book isn't about feelings.
It's about helping you get into action by replacing self-sabotaging thoughts that are messing with your progress. Ones that will
prevent you from your dream instead of propelling you toward it.
To do that effectively, you'll need to have the mindset that *God
has already been preparing you for what He's prepared for you.* And
it's wrapped up in that dream He's given you.

Whether you are running a business, creating a business, or wanting to do both, I'm here to help you answer the question, "Do you *mean* business when it comes to defining and aligning it with that God-given dream of yours?"

Before picking up this book, maybe you've had moments where you think that your dream is long gone. Like you had your chance and you missed it. But now, after all this God-given dream talk, you realize—or at least acknowledge—that maybe *something* is still there. Something that you can't quite put your finger on or define exactly. You wonder if whatever *it* is, could it be the thing that's keeping you from feeling whole? Remember, there is no empty space in you that God doesn't already know about or have a plan, strategy, and process ready to fill and make you whole.

It's often the thing you're continually pushing to the back of your mind because of time, finances, feelings, or a season of life. Sure, you may have dabbled in it here and there, maybe even got it mixed in and up with previous ventures. Maybe you do know what it is, but you haven't yet made it a primary focus so it keeps nagging at you in the recesses of your mind.

You now begin to look more closely at any nagging, lurking, or hovering "what if" questions like:

- What if I *did* pursue that crazy idea?
- What if now *is* the time?
- What if I *believed* this is what I was meant to do?

Those very questions are the ones that nagged, lurked, and hovered over me *for years.* And do you know what I finally came to realize? God is patiently waiting on us to understand that the connection between His dream *for us* is the very dream He's given *to us*!

GOD IS PATIENTLY WAITING ON US TO REALIZE THAT THE CONNECTION BETWEEN HIS DREAM FOR US IS THE VERY DREAM HE'S GIVEN TO US!

The moment you decide to connect those dots for yourself is the day you are right on time.

TIMING

God sees, He knows, and He's got your dream planned *for you*. It's been prepared and the process set out; you just need to answer His call and recognize that it's time. Time for you to explore, experiment, and recognize the calls pointing you closer and closer to the dream that was imagined by the Creator just *for you*.

Yes, you've likely already spent years building, creating, or pursuing other things. As a matter of fact, those actually helped you!

Are the wheels turning in your mind right now? I get it if you're thinking, "Nah, this is dumb. Nice try, but I'm not buying whatever it is you're selling here, sister."

That's fine, you can keep buying and borrowing others' doubts and opinions. You can continue to literally buy the reasons why "their way" is the better way to "the" dream life. You can keep following their lead to the generic dream, one that leaves everyone in a perpetual state of competition and comparison. I, too, was one who bought into "the" dream life over my specifically designed, God-given one. But not anymore!

Will you have the courage to step out? Out of:

- The fear of others' opinions,
- Fear of failure,
- Fear of a lack of qualifications.

Believe me when I tell you that I totally understand those fears. But will you believe that if I can step out, you can, too? C'mon, you got this and I'm right here with you!

The fact that you're still reading indicates that you're in the right place, and you're right on time.

You're not too young, too old, too busy, or too late. Your dream is not dumb or too far-fetched—and it's certainly not dead.

You may feel like it's dead or even mostly dead at times, but it's not. Like Miracle Max would say, "There's a big difference between all dead and mostly dead ... Mostly dead is slightly alive!" (C'mon, where are my *Princess Bride* movie peeps?) Your dream just needs some CPR, remember? Core values, Prioritizing, and Resources.

You absolutely can and should pursue *your* God-given dream. After all, you're smart and savvy (okay, probably a bit sassy, too), and VAL, you've already done so much *with* and *in* your life!

Is something in you beginning to spark? Maybe your emotions are hovering somewhere between excitement and doubt. Trust me, I know the pull between going "all in" one minute and thinking "why bother" the next. You know, why bother because someone else is already doing your dream ... or because by the time you learn what's required of you, you'll probably be 100! Random self-sabotaging thoughts like that are often followed by the temptation to just give up. But I encourage you to hang with me here and let's keep going together.

A STEP BACK IN TIME

In January 2010, I was invited to a neighbor's direct sales party. You know, one of those get-togethers where a salesperson shows up with all her wares from the company so you can buy directly from her, concluding with, "but wait—here's more!"

At that time, I was remarried to my amazingly supportive, handsome, hero of a husband (yep, still smitten) for about two-and-a-half years, had a one-year-old son from that marriage, and two young daughters from my previous marriage. My life was humming along as a wife and mother. I was living in a beautiful house, in a great neighborhood, with a nice car and all. of. the. things.

Now, don't think that my life was absent of drama, hurts, or even heartaches—life's messy, remember? (Just building up this beginning for you.)

Well, in case you didn't see this coming (neither did I), the party concluded with me joining the company as a rep, too! (Eye roll … I know, but hear me out.) You see, it was the perfect solution: For the price of joining the company, I got most of the things on my wish list and the *one* thing I really wanted came as a bonus! That's a win-win, right? Long story short, I became what was known in the industry as a "kit-napper."

The success, sisterhood, or career I could build or have by being a part of this company was of little interest to me. I had no intentions of booking, selling, or recruiting anyone. Period. Besides, my life was great! Wasn't it?

THE DREAM LIFE AWAITS

Fast forward to my first call from my upline director after completing a questionnaire she had sent me. It was about my dream life. Wait, what? What on earth does my dream life have to do with kit-napping? I was just being savvy and budget conscious. (Okay, maybe a little slick, too.) But what would it hurt to fill out the survey? I'm curious, so I go all in and answer questions such as, "If time and money were of no concern, what would you do and who would you help?" followed by, "How that would make you *feel*?"

Since I wasn't drinking the Kool-Aid at this point, I continued to let my mind wander as I answered the questions. What *would* I do with ridiculous amounts of money each month and the time to spend it?

During my conversation with the director, she shared that the opportunity wasn't just about making money and friends, but also what the money could *do*.

None of it was computing with me until I heard the word that immediately brought my wandering mind back to attention: incentives. Then another word: recognition.

Wait. Back up. My competitive self wanted to know more about these incentives and recognition. I already felt like I had won with my kit-napping tactic; now I could "win" more stuff ... for free *and* be publicly recognized for it? Sign me up!

Since I wasn't in it for the money, already had an amazing life with my family, loved Jesus and He loved me, I wasn't really seeing a connection between how being in direct sales would help me live my dream life. I was *already* living my dream life. But the allure of winning free stuff and being recognized for my efforts, that's what hooked me.

I'm not proud to admit this is how my entrepreneurial journey began, but that's how it started. Don't judge; just keep reading.

THIS DREAM IS ON!

I have no idea why anyone booked parties with me those first few weeks. My "approach" (we'll call it that) was brutally honest and probably borderline rude.

Want to know what I said at my launch party? My spiel went something like this: "Order whatever you want. I'm just doing this to win free stuff. And once I earn all of it, I'm out. So don't worry about me bugging you to buy, book, or join. I'm just earning these incentives and then quitting."

Guess what? They didn't care. They bought what they wanted, booked their own parties, and went on with their lives. Want to know what I said at their parties? The same thing I said at my own launch party! (Palm to face.)

Regardless, I earned those incentives in my first three months or thirty days, I don't even remember now. People continued to buy, book, and even join my team. "Ha! How funny is that?" I thought. Now I was the one with a team. More importantly to me at that time, I earned a place in my director's monthly newsletter right under the words, "Woo! Hoo!" Affirmation of my awesomeness in front of others? Yes, please.

Why am I sharing all of this? Because it's true. Plus, it's important for me to remember and for you to see how God used my greed in order to recognize others' needs. So, if a little of my humiliation helps you see Him a little better, I'm all for it.

EXIT IS THIS WAY

Now before you think this is some reverse psychology advice for those of you in direct sales, please read this carefully—I do *not* recommend this approach. However, I do recommend that you be authentic and truthful, which clearly, I was.

Here's what surprised me at the end of my incentive-earning period: I discovered I couldn't quit. Rather, I didn't want to quit. (I know; I couldn't believe it, either. But not for the reasons you may be thinking.)

What was wrong with me?! The kit-napping was good, and the incentives and recognition were surprisingly great bonuses. I had gotten more than I signed up for and according to my plan, it was time to go.

But something was happening; some type of shift. What was it? Turns out that it was more than a perspective shift; my very mission began to shift. You see, after the first few parties, I saw women who were brilliant, intelligent, fun, loving, and All. The. Things. But many of them were feeling tired, hurt, discouraged, overworked, overwhelmed, and struggling. These women were struggling financially, relationally, some physically, and many spiritually.

Now, suddenly, my mission wasn't just about me and my goal to get free stuff and recognition, it had become more about those tired, overwhelmed, underappreciated, and struggling women.

Now, instead of quitting, I was challenging myself. I wanted to be sure that every woman who came to one of these parties felt seen, heard, and cared about. The desire became about creating an atmosphere where they could be themselves and drop whatever it was that was burdening them, even if it was just for a little while.

It was also about the fun and the prizes! Oh, I was all about the prizes and making sure everyone had the chance to win *something!* I was having so much fun with it, too. The best part for me was that the company I represented was faith-based. So that gave me the "excuse" to weave in conversations of biblical encouragement. I had inspiring Scripture verse bookmarks with my info on the back as my first business cards.

REALITY CHECK

This shift in focus served my "business" very well (I use quotes here because that's what I was supposed to call it). I even started bragging about it because I now had a steadily growing customer base, a team of women nationwide, and extra money at the end of the month. In fact, my husband wasn't too sad to learn I made enough to cover both the car payment and the kids' private-school tuition. (He didn't mind the free incentive trip, either.)

But the truth was, I had no idea what it really meant to have and run a business! The company took care of my website, set up and tracked my email list, provided great marketing and advertising, and sent me a W-2 at the end of the year.

What I had was a steadily growing social media group, scheduled parties, consistent sales, and new recruits each month. Yes, I was a bit more creative and personal than that, but my point is, it wasn't really my own business.

Why did this bother me? Was this some type of conviction? Was I doing something wrong?

Somewhere along the line, I stopped believing in my definition of success. The one that had me showing up and making sure that women felt good about who they were and what they were doing. The success that had me making enough money to be more generous, and offering women the opportunity to do the same.

Instead, I began chasing what the company and industry itself deemed as success. Suddenly, if I was not at the top of the compensation plan with the title to go along with it, what was I even doing? With mounting frustration, I realized I merely had a decent hobby that helped women buy products, have fun, and join the company, not a business of my own or the ever-elusive dream career I was apparently supposed to have.

The fear of being "less than" also began to creep in, along with doubt that what I was doing wasn't good enough. A new focus began to take root.

I became obsessed with numbers, members, sales, titles, and promotions. I was determined to build a successful business, even if I had to suck all the fun out of it!

Oh, how I wish that weren't true. This is yet another part that I'd like to exclude from this book, but I want to keep it real. Show the mess I was in—and even created—because of others' pressure and opinions.

At what point did I buy into the belief that my business was the end-all, be-all for my freedom, security, status, and ultimately my success? Wasn't I already happy with my life? Didn't God already define who I am?

LETTING "IT" GO

Is any of this resonating with you? Maybe you have a similar story to mine. Or yours is about being hell-bent on proving something to yourself or someone else. After all, that's another way to climb your way to the top of our culture's recognized form of success, isn't it?

I spent eight-and-a-half years in the direct sales industry with the same company. The first few years were on a mission to help women have fun and see their value. The next few were a mix of competitive corporate climbing and coaching (I'm not as proud of the competitive climbing part as I am of the coaching). Coaching women, whether on my team or someone else's, to use direct sales as a vehicle to achieve *their* definition of success was impactful. I felt like I was making some kind of difference in their lives, even if they left my team or the company in order to pursue it (which many did).

It was during this time I sensed that God had something else in store for me. Something bigger, beyond what I could do or become within that company.

Another keeping-it-real confession: I'd like to say I asked for clarification and trusted His prompting. I'd like to say that I figured it out immediately and moved right along. But I didn't.

Instead, I worked very hard to convince both myself and God that I could hang on to my good thing—the thing that *I* had built (and by industry standards, was quite successful at in regard to rank, title, and income)—while at the same time starting on this new thing, one He was pointing me toward.

Now, I will encourage and advise you all day long to build your side hustle while still relying on the stability of your main job. But this was not what I was supposed to be doing. It became very clear to me that it was time to let go. Let go of *my* good thing in order to receive what God had in store. For *three years* I tried to convince Him that I could do both. Until I finally realized I couldn't and let go.

Letting go sounds somewhat noble, but not in my case. This was like a fierce tug-of-war. The kind where your hands hurt so bad that you *have* to let go. Yeah, it was that kind of letting go for me; it wasn't pretty. I pray that you don't wait that long when God prompts you to let go of your good thing in order for you to experience His *better* thing.

It was only then, at the point of exhaustion and surrender, that I was able to begin piecing together a real definition of success. One that was personal, intentional, and uniquely meant for me.

REDEFINING SUCCESS

Many people fall into thinking that money is the only problem-solver when it comes to defining success and living your dream. I've come to realize, however, that money is a medium to exchange, not a solution. (We'll talk more about these later.) You can be successful and significant with or without money.

So it's important to define what you are falling for, and the reason you're falling for it when it comes to your definition of success and your dream. That answer could be what's preventing you from recognizing your dream as opposed to someone else's idea of your dream. Defining your starting point is important so that you can level up effectively because you're well-informed and ready, not because you're pressured or full of FOMO (fear of missing out), which today's marketing is so good at instigating.

Any version or definition of success that has you pursuing a dream that's not aligned with the one God has for you is the exact reason why you end up feeling broken, busted, and disgusted, whether it's financially, relationally, physically, or even spiritually.

The unrealized dream often causes you to repeat the cycle because you have been convinced *you* must have done something wrong. So you buy another book, join another direct sales or MLM company, or go to another conference, doctor, seminar, gym, or church in search of whatever "it" is that you must have missed. By this point, you're just feeling it's all wrong!

THERE IS NO MAGIC FORMULA, NO BOOK, EXPERT GURU, OR COURSE THAT IS GOING TO DEFINE YOU.

What will strengthen you, fulfill you, and enable you to make an impact is already waiting for you; you just need to believe God when He tells you where to find it!

VAL, God sees you and so do I. But your ability to believe that is between you and Him. Along my journey with Him so far, I've learned that success is a perspective, not a destination.

> *Success is a perspective,*
> *not a destination.*

I'm no expert or famous guru, just an explorer on the way to my dream that God planted, prompted and is continually pointing me toward. By sharing my journey, I invite you to see what I've defined, discovered, and determined to do along the way. Know that I'm still working on embracing my own VAL status too.

Remember: Broken, busted, and disgusted are feelings, not sentences to be served. It's time for each of us to trade those heart hurts, aches, and breaks for the hallelujahs of becoming strengthened, fulfilled, and impactful VALs (Valued, Amazing Ladies).

VAL, let's show this world who we are!

CHAPTER 3

Who Are You?

DO YOU KNOW WHO YOU REALLY ARE?

Maybe it's an odd thing to question who someone thinks they are, beyond the context of calling someone out on their rudeness, but I think it's a powerful question. It's one that is often overlooked and rarely asked sincerely, especially of ourselves.

So, who are you? I mean really, beyond the roles, titles, or labels you've been given or assigned. I'm talking about the "you" that extends beyond even your history. Yeah, *that* you.

Sure, it's easy to rattle off what you do for a living or what's got the majority of your attention in this season of life, who means the most to you, as well as where you've been and how you got to where you are now. With some coaxing, I'm confident you'd even share what it is that you wish for and ultimately hope to accomplish in life. These answers roll pretty effortlessly off the tongue, but they still don't get to the heart of the question, "Who are you?"

Whew! Suddenly this "Who are you?" becomes a loaded question. One that quickly has you self-consciously assessing your audience so you can offer the best, most acceptable response.

YOU'VE GOT TO BE BEFORE YOU CAN DO, AND DO BEFORE YOU CAN HAVE.

— Zig Ziglar

See how slippery this slope gets when you neglect to take the time to determine for yourself who you are?

There's not much doubt who the current culture says you are … or should be. Its focus is on a me, myself, and I perspective. From the devices we carry to what we now call taking pictures of ourselves, is all about the products, promotions, or promises relating to personal gain. We may as well just call it the "i-culture," and I'm not just talking about a particular brand or company; the whole societal norm is quick to blur the lines between self-interest and another's best interest. We live in a culture that is quick to shine a light on self, but slow to show the Light of the World.

Why is one light vastly acceptable over *the Light*? Maybe because it's easier in our day-to-day to just go with the flow according to this "i-culture." Easier in the short-term, perhaps, but how's that working out long-term, especially when culture decides something else is better, more accepted, and expected?

How then, as believers, do we effectively live *in* the world without being *of* the world as is the standard we are so often told and held to by our own Christian culture? How do we embrace and use things like technology without being consumed, confined, or corrupted by it?

The short answer is: Know who you are. But as I'm sure you're already starting to realize, there's more to uncover and understand here.

WHO YOU REALLY ARE MATTERS

You've got to settle this question for yourself: Who are you? Yes, we've already established that you are valued, amazing, and loved, but you are also so much more.

IF WE CLAIM THAT WE EXPERIENCE A SHARED LIFE WITH HIM AND CONTINUE TO STUMBLE AROUND IN THE DARK, WE'RE OBVIOUSLY LYING THROUGH OUR TEETH- WE'RE NOT LIVING WHAT WE CLAIM. BUT IF WE WALK IN THE LIGHT, GOD HIMSELF BEING THE LIGHT, WE ALSO EXPERIENCE A SHARED LIFE WITH ONE ANOTHER, AS THE SACRIFICED BLOOD OF JESUS, GOD'S SON, PURGES ALL OUR SIN.

- 1 John 1:6-7 MSG

Here's a look at my own answers to this question. My hope is that it will help you begin to see how the process unfolds when it comes to defining who *you* are.

- I'm a Jesus follower, wife, mother of three, volunteer, founder, entrepreneur, speaker, reader, writer, daughter, sister, and friend.
- I'm in my final years of being a p-uber driver (aka Mom Taxi ... parent-Uber—get it?)
- Some more colorful descriptors of my individuality include being divorced, a ministry outcast, and often a legalism disruptor.
- I'm an energetic talker, passionate encourager, trucker-hat, and sneakers-wearing girl.
- In a nutshell, I'm a curly-haired MESSterpiece pursuing God's heart in order to make progress on His *big* dream for me. The work is becoming the kind of VAL that can handle it!

This list could go on and on, as I'm sure is the case for you too, once you get the hang of it! Some of the examples reflect my current reality, some my history, and a few are the labels put on me by others. Many of those roles and titles I own proudly, some are generic, and others I'm still growing my faith in order to pursue more boldly.

The point is that when you can define and refine your own individual features, flaws, finishes, and unknown futures—everything else pretty much rolls right off your back, making forward focus much easier.

It's okay if you're not feeling all that confident about it just yet. Keep going and you'll get there.

GO AHEAD AND GIVE IT A GO FOR YOURSELF. WRITE WHATEVER COMES TO MIND WHEN YOU CONSIDER, "WHO ARE YOU?"

SHARED IDENTITIES

Tucked within the pages of my Bible is a list of words that remind me of who I am in Christ Jesus. This list reminds me of the truth when

- the days get too hard;
- I feel unseen, unheard, or even unloved;
- others try to tell me who they think I should be or try to become;
- I lose my steam or any sliver of courage.

The list comes from Ephesians 1:3–14 and is just as much for you as for me. I encourage you to personalize these truths by stating "I am" before each one.

BLESSED	REDEEMED	FILLED WITH THE HOLY SPIRIT
CHOSEN	FORGIVEN	
HOLY	RICH IN GOD'S GRACE	GUARANTEED OUR INHERITANCE
BLAMELESS	INCLUDED IN CHRIST	GOD'S POSSESSION
PREDESTINED		
ADOPTED	KNOWING THE TRUTH	THE PRAISE OF HIS GLORY
	SAVED	

These words are a reminder of who I am because of the gift of salvation; the gift of Christ exchanging His life for mine. I don't know about you, but living through the lens of who He says I am is much less stressful than trying to live a perfect life! This is why I love this reminder list so much—we're called to live purposefully, not perfectly.

Maybe you're thinking I'm getting way too "out there" for you. Or this all sounds too fluffy and not practical for everyday real life. *Your* everyday real life.

The foundational stuff is always the hardest to work through, and you can't ignore or go around it. The best way to the other side is always through it. I encourage you to keep reading and try the activities to discover exactly how relevant it really is to your life.

TIME TO MAKE A DECISION

What happens when you want something to change? You make a decision. Either you decide to do something about it, or you ignore that desire for change, and *nothing changes*. Both are decisions.

The same is true about deciding to find out *and own* who God made you to be. When you finally get tired of wearing the labels, picking up (or being handed) your history, and ready to quit carrying the titles or roles that weigh you down, a decision needs to be made.

You can choose to stay where you are (wandering) while wondering if this is the life you were meant for or ... decide to believe who God says you are and trust Him for direction in becoming that person.

I can feel you thinking: "Where do I even start?" (Am I right?)

The answer: Just begin one step at a time. Even if you don't know *where* you're going right now, you'll at least know *who* you need to be in order to get there. At some point in defining who you are, you'll come to realize that deciding who you need to be becomes quite helpful and powerful!

Ponder that for a second, *who you need to be* .... It can be easy to skip over that part without ever giving much thought to whether I'm who I need to be in order to handle

- what it is that I really want,
- what's been entrusted to me, and
- the obstacles and opposition that I know will get in my way.

We get so caught up in the to-dos of our lives that we often forget to put importance on who we are actually becoming.

Life isn't about trying to fit in, it's about stepping into your right fit.

Take some time to ponder who you are and who you are becoming. Are you okay with your answers? If not, what decisions need to be made?

Once you are able to get some clarity on who you were made to be (beyond titles, labels, and your history), you start to become a powerful decision-maker. Who doesn't want that?

Decisions provide direction.

Did you catch that? Most of us live the opposite way—unable to make a decision until we get some direction! But the reality is much different.

GETTING TO THE CORE OF YOU

Despite your current circumstance or past situations, you're heading in a definite direction: your future. While unpredictable, it's still important and requires attention and intention. You're going to end up there no matter what, so wouldn't it be amazing to show up as the person you would want to be in your future?

Don't get hung up on how you're seen now or have been known in the past, but instead focus on becoming the shining testament of who you were meant to be all along!

One of the first things I help my clients do is define their core values. Why? Because what you value directly impacts your thoughts and actions, which eventually affect your future.

So now that I've teed up this portion of the chapter for you, we're going to dive right into the same exercise I walk those clients through. You, too, are going to dig past the common and shared ones (e.g., faith, family, health, impact, etc.) to those that reflect *your* core values! Getting gut honest with yourself is never easy or comfortable, but it's been proven time and time again to be worth the work in the end.

If you're not a write-in-your-book kind of VAL, now would be the time to grab a pen and paper.

Here's how it works: The next several pages are full of words. Lots of words. Each word represents a value. You are going to compile your own list of words based on if it holds value to you. If it does, circle it or note it. Your list can be as long as you want (for now). Don't overthink it. If a word you see resonates or holds some type of value to you, it makes the list—it's your list.

STEP 1: CIRCLE ALL OF THE WORDS THAT RESONATE WITH YOU

If you're hesitant about a word, just go with your gut. If it is important to you, circle it. As you look at each word, ask yourself how and why that word resonates with you.

TIP: Insert a word from the list into the following statements to help you determine if it's valuable enough to be placed on *your* list:

It is important to me to have [value word].

It means a lot to me when a person has/does [value word].

I could not live in a world without [value word].

If a word that you feel is important to you isn't included on this list, by all means, add it! This is definitely a good start in helping you begin to define *your* core values.

ACCEPTANCE	TO DETAIL	CLEANLINESS
ACCESSIBILITY	ATTENTIVE	CLEAR
ACCOMPLISHMENT	AVAILABILITY	CLEAR-MINDED
ACCOUNTABILITY	AWARENESS	CLEVER
ACCURACY	BALANCE	COLLABORATION
ACHIEVEMENT	BEAUTY	COMFORT
ACTIVITY	BEING THE BEST	COMMITMENT
ADAPTABILITY	BELONGING	COMMON SENSE
ADVENTUROUS	BOLDNESS	COMMUNICATION
AFFECTION	BRAVERY	COMMUNITY
AGGRESSIVE	BRILLIANCE	COMPASSION
AGILITY	CALM	COMPETENCE
ALERTNESS	CAPABLE	COMPETITION
AMBITION	CAREFUL	COMPETITIVE
AMUSEMENT	CARING	COMPLETION
ANTI-CORPORATE	CERTAINTY	COMPOSURE
ANTICIPATION	CHALLENGE	COMPREHENSIVE
APPRECIATION	CHANGE	CONCENTRATION
APPROACHABLE	CHARACTER	CONFIDENCE
ASSERTIVE	CHARITY	CONFIDENTIALITY
ATTENTION	CHEERFUL	CONFORMITY

CONNECTION	EMPATHY	FRIENDLY
CONSCIOUSNESS	ENCOURAGEMENT	FRUGALITY
CONSISTENCY	ENDURANCE	FUN
CONTENTMENT	ENERGY	GIVING
CONTRIBUTION	ENGAGEMENT	GLOBAL
CONTROL	ENJOYMENT	GRATITUDE
CONVICTION	ENTERTAINMENT	GROWTH
COOPERATION	ENTHUSIASM	GUIDANCE
CORRECT	ENTREPRENEURSHIP	HAPPINESS
COURAGE	ENVIRONMENT	HARD WORK
COURTESY	EQUALITY	HARMONY
CRAFTINESS	ETHICAL	HEALTH
CRAFTSMANSHIP	EXCELLENCE	HEART
CREATIVITY	EXCITING	HELPFUL
CREDIBILITY	EXPERIENCE	HISTORY
CURIOSITY	EXPERTISE	HOLINESS
DARING	EXPLORATION	HONESTY
DECISIVE	EXPRESSIVE	HONOR
DEPENDABILITY	EXTROVERT	HOPEFUL
DEPTH	FAIRNESS	HOSPITALITY
DETERMINED	FAITH	HUMBLE
DEVOTION	FAMILY	HUMOR
DIFFERENT	FASHION	HYGIENE
DIRECT	FAST	IMAGINATION
DISCIPLINE	FEARLESS	IMPACT
DISCOVERY	FIRM	IMPARTIAL
DRIVE	FITNESS	INDEPENDENCE
DUTY	FLEXIBLE	INDIVIDUALITY
EAGERNESS	FLUENCY	INDUSTRY
EDUCATION	FOCUS	INFORMAL
EFFECTIVE	FORMAL	INNOVATIVE
EFFICIENT	FREEDOM	INQUISITIVE
ELEGANCE	FRESH	INSIGHTFUL

INSPIRATION	MYSTERY	PREPARED
INTEGRITY	NEATNESS	PRESERVATION
INTELLIGENCE	NERVE	PRIDE
INTENSITY	NOBLE	PRIVACY
INTERNATIONAL	NOTICEABLE	PROACTIVE
INTUITION	NUTRITION	PRODUCTIVE
INTUITIVE	OPEN	PROFESSIONAL
INVENTION	OPEN-MINDED	PROFITABLE
INVESTING	OPTIMISM	PROGRESS
INVITING	ORDER	PROSPERITY
JOY	ORGANIZATION	PUNCTUALITY
JUSTICE	ORIGINALITY	PURITY
KINDNESS	PARTNERSHIP	PURSUIT
KNOWLEDGE	PASSION	QUALITY
LEADERSHIP	PATIENCE	RATIONAL
LIBERTY	PATRIOTISM	REAL
LISTENING	PEACE	RECOGNITION
LIVELY	PEOPLE	RECREATION
LOCAL	PERCEPTIVE	REFINED
LOGIC	PERFORMANCE	RELIABLE
LONGEVITY	PERSEVERANCE	RESILIENCE
LOVE	PERSISTENCE	RESOURCEFUL
LOYALTY	PERSONAL DEVELOPMENT	RESPECT
MASTERY		RESPONSIBLE
MATURITY	PERSONAL GROWTH	RESPONSIVE
MAXIMIZING	PERSUASIVE	REST
MEANING	PHILANTHROPY	RESTRAINT
MELLOW	PLAYFULNESS	RESULTS
METICULOUS	PLEASANTNESS	REVERENCE
MINDFUL	POPULARITY	RISK TAKING
MODERATION	POSITIVE	SACRIFICE
MODESTY	POWERFUL	SAFETY
MOTIVATION	PRACTICAL	SANITARY
	PRECISE	

SATISFACTION

SECURITY

SELF-AWARENESS

SELF-CONTROL

SELF-MOTIVATION

SELF-RELIANCE

SELF-RESPONSIBILITY

SELFLESS

SENSE OF HUMOR

SENSITIVITY

SERENITY

SERIOUS

SERVICE

SHARING

SIGNIFICANCE

SILENCE

SILLINESS

SIMPLICITY

SINCERITY

SKILL

SMART

SOLITUDE

SPEED

SPIRIT

SPIRITUALITY

SPONTANEOUS

STABILITY

STATUS

STEALTH

STEWARDSHIP

STRENGTH

STRUCTURE

SUCCEED

SUCCESS

SUPPORT

SURPRISE

SUSTAINABILITY

SYMPATHY

SYNERGY

SYSTEMIZATION

TALENT

TEAMWORK

THANKFUL

THOROUGH

THOUGHTFUL

TIMELY

TOLERANCE

TOUGH

TRADITIONAL

TRANQUIL

TRANSPARENCY

TRUSTWORTHY

TRUTH

UNDERSTANDING

UNFLAPPABLE

UNIQUE

UNIVERSAL

USEFUL

UTILITY

VALOR

VARIETY

VICTORIOUS

VIGOR

VIRTUE

VISION

VITALITY

WARMTH

WATCHFUL

WEALTH

WELCOMING

WILLFULNESS

WISDOM

WONDER

WORK/LIFE BALANCE

WORLDWIDE

Okay, by now your list is probably pretty long and you may find yourself encouraged by all the things you deem important to you (as you should be, especially if you have never done an exercise like this before).

You are feeling good because those words hold value; they mean something to you and it's exciting to see them compiled together!

The cool thing is that even though some of us may have the same words on our list, it doesn't make us the same. It just means we both appreciate or hold similar values in certain areas of our lives. *It's how we live out these values that make us so beautifully and uniquely different.*

But ... as good as it feels to take some personalized action, we are going to do a bit of purging next. That collection of meaningful words was just a beginning; a baseline for narrowing down *what really matters.*

Now take a look at your compiled list and pare it down to just ten words. And ... go! (Cue the *Jeopardy!* music.)

STEP 2: NARROW YOUR VALUES LIST TO 10

Got those? Good. Take a minute to look them over and let them sink in. Allow them to infiltrate your emotions for a few minutes. Do any of them stand out more than others? Can you feel some clarity beginning to formulate in your mind?

Well, I hate to break up your wonderful daydream, but you're not quite finished yet. Now you are going to take that list of ten and pare it down to just five. Ideally, you'd take it down to just three, but this may be your first time at this, so we'll stick to five for now. But I do challenge you at some point to take it down to just three, if you can.

This is the last purge. Don't poop out on me now; I promise we are going somewhere that is worth the effort.

STEP 3: TAKE YOUR VALUES LIST TO 5

ADVANCED STEP: TAKE IT TO 3 IF YOU CAN

Here's a little help if you need it: When comparing similar words, decide on the one that resonates *most*. Look up the meanings of these words and see if one definition hits you in the feels more than the other. Sometimes a synonym of a word actually works better than the few you're struggling to choose between.

Don't be tempted to skip this part. I know it seems like a lot, but think about this:

> *If you aren't willing to take the time to uncover your core values, then you'll be tempted to chase or adopt others' values.*

Wouldn't you rather pour your energy into things that align with who *you* were made to be?

Maybe you are thinking that you'll read the whole book first, then come back and do this exercise later. Fair enough; I hope that you do. And I pray that *when you do*, it becomes a resource and a reference to remind you of *your* core values.

FINAL STEP: WRITE DOWN YOUR 5 TOP CORE VALUES

CORE VALUE	SYNONYMS	WHY THIS RESONATES/ MATTERS

**ANYTHING EXTRA THAT YOU'D LIKE TO NOTE/
REMEMBER ABOUT THIS EXERCISE?**

WORKING IT OUT IN REAL LIFE

When I did this for the first time, I had an awful time narrowing down my list. I love words! The more the better, right? But I forged ahead and kept looking up words and reading their definitions. It came down to multiple words battling for the last spot on my list that I wanted narrowed down to just three core values. I already had purpose and authenticity as my first two, but now for that third and final spot, I was torn between kindness, flexibility, and grace. They were equally of value to me. How could I choose?!

I finally settled on grace because it encompasses both kindness and flexibility. After this exercise, my core values became authenticity, purpose, and grace. Authenticity points to my personality and the convicting challenge to always "keep it real." Purpose reminds me to always take into account the why behind the action I'm about to embark on. Grace, well, that is the glue that keeps me all together. It's also an indicator and reminder to be as generous with it as much as I need it in return!

Today, these values continue to be my North Star, keeping me focused and at the core behind all that I aspire to become and do. Yours can do that for you, too.

YOUR FOUNDATION

We haven't talked much about your dream in this chapter, but I hope you'll see the connection that who you are is as unique and important as your core values. *It's what will hold up your dream, time and time again.*

Determining those three to five words, while tough, was important. Those are now the filter through which you'll make decisions, the reason behind your actions, and increase or decrease your interactions.

Your core values help you make better decisions, define boundaries, and ensure that you work on the right things at the right time.

CORE VALUES KEEP YOU FOCUSED ON THE RIGHT DREAM-YOURS.

The next time you struggle to make a decision, define a boundary, or determine what project to focus on, ask yourself: Does this align with who God says I am *and* my core values?

THE STRUGGLE IS REAL

Every day there are struggles—life's messy, remember? But our perspectives can make all the difference. *Learn to accept that the struggle isn't about yes and no answers. It's about making the choice between good and better.*

Your core values are just the ticket to get you out of this jam, especially when you're not sure if a tough choice is *pulling you away* or *pushing you toward* your dream. Run that tough choice through your list of core values!

Remember mine? Authenticity, purpose, and grace. Real-life examples are always helpful, so here's mine for you.

My scenarios usually go a little something like this, and for immediate relevance, we'll use this book as my "tough decision":

> **CORE VALUE QUESTION:** Does this book (choice) allow you to be authentically (core value) you?
> **ME:** Yes.

> **CORE VALUE:** How does it accomplish this? (Or "why not?" if the answer is "no.")
> **ME:** My goal is to inform and equip as many women as I can that they are Valued Amazing Ladies and their dream is waiting on them. And since I already love to write, a book allows me to speak to countless VALs in a way that honors each other's time.

CORE VALUE: What's the purpose (core value) behind writing this book (choice)?
ME: It's twofold:

1. I've always wanted to be a public speaker. Several years ago, God shared a vision with me for what He had in store for me. It blew me away! But after years of trying to accomplish this on my own, to no avail, that exciting dream He had for me was fading. Until ... He revealed through Psalm 45:1 that writing is a form of speaking.

2. Now I can see that through writing, and in this case, a book, helps me live that dream of public speaking. Just not in the way I had expected. It was actually better. Because now I can "speak" in a way and at a pace that I can manage and is easily accessible and affordable to those who choose to "hear" what God's put on my heart to share.

CORE VALUE: Who will benefit most from writing a book (choice)? (i.e., will it benefit you or others?)
ME: I pray that it's both! The goal of the book is to help as many VALs as possible realize that their dream is meant for them. God absolutely has a plan and purpose for that dream in their heart. So by sharing what I've learned, I get to live out my dream on purpose with purpose! I'd say that checks the core value decision filter.

CORE VALUE: Who will need to show the most grace (core value) if you write this book (choice)?

ME: Everyone will have to show grace. Me to myself during my perfection-turned-paralysis moments. My family for the time it takes me away from them to do the writing. To my readers, who may have too-high expectations from me as a writer (first book, y'all).

YOUR TURN, VAL

What big decision is weighing on you right now? Which choice hangs in the balance between "good" and "better"? Notice I didn't ask a yes or no question. We know how those typically turn out. We too often say "yes" out of our people-pleasing habits instead of the "no" we should have uttered in the first place!

 **PRIORITIZED FOCUS PRACTICE: ALIGN WHO GOD SAYS YOU ARE WITH YOUR CORE VALUES TO HELP YOU MAKE BETTER DECISIONS.**

VAL, does [this choice] align with who you are as well as support [your core value]?

How so?

VAL, what's [the core value] behind [this choice]?

Who will benefit most from [this choice]?

VAL, who will have to show/be/do the most work surrounding [this core value] if you make [this choice]?

Are you okay with that?

You may have to tweak the questions a bit depending on your core value and the choice you're weighing, but I have confidence you understand how this works. Most importantly, I hope you use it as a tool to filter and sift through those tough questions as they come up.

Now that we've gotten to the core of *you*, let's ditch the excess baggage of titles, achievements, and labels, particularly the ones holding you back. It's time for the real you to begin flexing your core values as a way to embrace the journey ahead!

THE DAY OUR MEMORIES BECOME LARGER THAN OUR DREAMS IS THE DAY OUR SOUL BEGINS TO SHRINK.

– Ike Reighard

CHAPTER 4

What *Is* the Dream?

GOD IS PREPPING YOU FOR WHAT HE HAS ALREADY *prepared for you*. Whether or not you believe that statement makes all the difference in what you'll do next ... and just how effective those next steps will be. When it comes to your dream, you might not believe that it's there, waiting on you. You might think that you need to imagine it and then create it. But God has already imagined and created it for you.

Faith means believing in advance what will only make sense in reverse.

- PHILIP YANCEY

When I found this quote, it was a big a-ha moment, one that really put the sentiment about how God's prepping you for what He's already prepared *for you,* into perspective.

As believers, we are often given many definitions and versions of what faith is or *should* look like. While hearing about others' faith can be great guides, it's so important for you to measure what you learn from others about *your faith* so that you are able to discern the basis of it *for yourself* and align those beliefs and actions with God's Word. Otherwise, you may end up feeling more confused and unsure instead of gaining the clarity and strength you were looking for.

By continuing to mature in your relationship with God through studying His Word, you begin to reach a better understanding of what faith looks like. Yet, even with this knowledge, there can still be a sense of mystery about how faith, the future, and your experiences all fit together.

Don't worry, it's not uncommon to feel that way; we all do at times. That's why it's so important to understand the role your present faith has in shaping your future. When your faith is strong and reflects what God says about who you are and where He's

YOUR FUTURE IS DEPENDENT ON YOUR PRESENT FAITH, WHICH GIVES YOU THE ABILITY TO MAKE SENSE OF YOUR PERSONAL HISTORY.

taking you, then your past experiences begin to make sense. You'll recognize how they prepared you for your current situation. In other words, your future is dependent on your present faith, which gives you the ability to make sense of your personal history.

MAKING SENSE OF YOUR HISTORY

At one point in my childhood, I wanted to be a teacher. Well, at least I thought I did. Desks and chalkboards were some of my favorite toys to have around. (Today, they still are!) According to my report cards and detention slips, being talkative was one of my most common struggles. Later, after being told I was bossy, teaching was a profession I was *recommended* to pursue. To be fair, a high school English teacher told me I was a good writer and encouraged me to also "dig into that," which makes sense now.

When I was young, a school teacher was the only reference point for teaching. Today, of course, we know there are all kinds of teachers and teaching professions you can call your own.

Hindsight is 20/20, right? Speaking of 2020, the global pandemic was an interesting teacher, wasn't it? Suddenly, two of my children were learning virtually at home because of school shutdowns. I did what I could to help them, but I can honestly say that becoming a school teacher isn't even a blip on my dream job's radar.

Yet, God has me teaching. Not scholastic academics to children (and I thank Him for that), but guiding Christian women in business how to live in alignment with their God-given assignment. The preparation has taken years and in fact, *I'm still a student myself* of the methods and subjects I didn't know existed when I was younger.

Some find their calling very early on in life and know without a doubt it's what they were meant for and pursue it wholeheartedly. Awesome. Others of us begin to believe those people must be truly special, more so than us. We convince ourselves that our childhood dreams were just that: kid dreams. What on earth could they have to do with what we were meant for *now*?

ONE COMMON PURPOSE

God created us to share the good news of His love for others. That is our one common purpose as Christ followers. However, God created and designed us to have *a specific and unique way in which to carry out that purpose.* It's through the dream He put in our hearts. And he's been preparing and equipping us to succeed at that dream our whole life.

Yet we tend to overcomplicate it. We believe others' dreams are meant to be our dreams, often because we've been told that our dream is too big or unrealistic. That we are too young, too old, or that it's too soon or too late to pursue it. We tell ourselves that we are not equipped, educated, or empowered enough.

All the while, we can't seem to shake this nagging sense that we must have been meant for more than "this" life that we're doing right now. For crying out loud, we are smart, savvy (yes, even a bit sassy) women. Many have raised (or are raising) children while doing whatever it takes to meet everyone's needs and make ends meet. We are quick to support others, create environments of inclusiveness, and try our best to make it all work out (oh, and try to prioritize a workout, too).

I'm guessing that you tell your kids and even total strangers to go after their dreams, don't you? Then you work hard to support them. Yet, inside, maybe you feel guilty because you doubt anyone *really* gets to live their dream.

If anyone cared enough to ask what *your* dream was, you'd probably hold back the truth and instead say something like, "I know it's dumb, but I've always wanted to …" or "If it weren't so impossible, I'd probably be …."

> *Slowly you become the acceptable, expected version of yourself instead of the woman you once dared to dream you'd become.*

Maybe you allowed fear, doubt, and others' opinions to talk you out of your biggest dreams and goals. Worse, now you're unsure what your dream is/was anymore.

MAYBE IT'S ME

I'm not a conformist; I'm a realist.

I grew up in a legalistic environment. From the churches my brother and I attended to the private Christian schools my parents scraped and saved to send us to through high school. Those environments told me how to live, think, act, and even be, all "according to the Bible." This girl resists being told what to do and how to be, so I butted heads with *a lot* of those authorities. Throughout it all, I tried to understand how this believing, faith-ing, trusting, and obeying God "according the Bible" thing worked in real life … *my* real life.

Looking back, it's not that their view was wrong per se, just really heavy on judgment and blind obedience, according to their interpretation/understanding of Scripture. Now I can see that it lacked the balance of *the truth in love* with a side of mercy and grace, thank you very much. In other words, religion ruled more than the invitation to a personal relationship with God.

Whether that was their intention, belief, or something in the middle, that's how it was perceived, and I resisted. Yet, at the same time, I knew they weren't necessarily wrong; maybe it was their approach and delivery? At the time, I was too young and definitely lacked the faith experience to understand the difference; only they and God know that answer.

All I know is that after a religion-y upbringing and messy adult life, I was desperate to find what I was missing. By the time I had gone through my second divorce (high school "love" and a dose of religious legalism are not good foundations for a lasting marriage—in my case, the first lasted six months, and the second, just shy of eight years with two kids), I was at my wit's end trying to discover *what was wrong with me*. I was desperate to find my identity beyond the titles I gave myself, the labels others put on me, and definitely my history. My life was—you guessed it—a mess.

With nowhere to go but up, I became a voracious student of the Word. At one point, I even thought I would make a good Bible teacher! But that idea flew out the window because I mean, thanks to my upbringing, the only way a woman could teach biblical lessons was either in a children's Sunday school class or at a Christian school, right?

Nevertheless, by digging into God's Word, I was finding real solutions, comfort, guidance, and authority for how to handle my real-world problems and messy identity crisis. I discovered that the Bible's not for shaming, condemning, or manipulating. Who knew?! (That's totally sarcastic by the way—just maybe a little reflective trauma from my biblical past experiences.)

Why was no one openly talking about the solutions and answers I was finding on my own? Then again, it's not like I was fielding a lot of warm, welcoming invitations to come sit at tables to discuss my questions and find answers (which is why the coffee's always on and room at the table at my house). Even when I felt "safe enough" to ask a question, I didn't find anyone who was willing to dig into it *with me*. Nah, they were comfortable with the usual, acceptable answers like "pray about it," "read this book," and "there must be some sin blocking you from getting the answer."

That part of my history turned out to include some of my deepest, darkest times … but also became the catalyst for God to shine the brightest kind of light on just the parts He needed me to see, feel, understand, and apply.

PROOF IS TRUTH

I have found that proof is truth, and truth always finds a way to prove itself. Over the years, God's Word has proven itself true time and time again. *Even when I didn't want it to.*

I can tell you that there were times when the message was crystal clear and very much for me. But what did I do? I felt the need to spend hours scouring the Internet to see if it was true … according to someone else. I wanted to see if anyone had already written a book about it, experienced it, or lived to tell about it. This was how I justified procrastinating on doing what I *knew was for me*. (Remember the struggle of letting go of my "it" business in Chapter 2?)

SO DON'T BE MISLED,
DEAR BROTHERS. [AND
SISTERS!] BUT WHATEVER
IS GOOD AND PERFECT
COMES TO US FROM GOD,
THE CREATOR OF ALL
LIGHT, AND HE SHINES
FOREVER WITHOUT
CHANGE OR SHADOW. AND
IT WAS A HAPPY DAY FOR
HIM WHEN HE GAVE US
OUR NEW LIVES THROUGH
THE TRUTH OF HIS
WORD, AND WE BECAME,
AS IT WERE, THE FIRST
CHILDREN IN HIS NEW
FAMILY.

- James 1:16-18 TLB

Ultimately, it didn't matter what else I found out there because He already said it in there—His Word—for me, for you, for us. What I know now that I didn't know then was that those crystal-clear messages were from the Holy Spirit, who was stirring up what was already within me—God's Word.

Maybe you've been there, too: Hurt by religion and/or confused by what you have been or who you're told you are. Yet, deep down, you know there has got to be something else, something deeper, something *true*.

My prayer for you right now, VAL (Valued Amazing Lady), is that you stop claiming others' words for your life and that you find the courage to dig into finding the truth for yourself. Odds are, there are already clues. May my personal example be an encouragement to you.

YOUR DREAM

Remember the quote I shared at the beginning of this chapter, the one that was a huge a-ha for me? "Faith means believing in advance what will only make sense in reverse." Think where you've been, VAL. What you've been through. What you pictured yourself growing up to become. While none of us can change our past, we can allow ourselves to be informed by it.

I know that my past sure looks like a big ol' hot MESS (and I only shared a small part—oh, there's so much more mess), but I now understand that God used it to point me to my future. A future that exchanged my MESS for the MESSage He wants me to share.

How about you? Can you see how your past mess can be your MESSage now? I wish that I could cup your face, look you in the eye, and verbally say this next sentence to you:

Your past is meant to help change someone's future and it's con-nected to your dream. And VAL, get this: It's important and God has already planned for your MESSage to be effective.

FOR I KNOW THE THOUGHTS THAT I THINK TOWARD YOU, SAITH THE LORD, THOUGHTS OF PEACE, AND NOT OF EVIL, TO GIVE YOU AN EXPECTED END.

– Jeremiah 29:11 KJV

YOUR HOPE FOR A FUTURE

Will you dream with me for a moment? I mean, really dream *big*. Yes, you probably think it's a little corny, just as I did back when I was a kit-napper in that direct sales company. But you and I have some shared history now; we've done some work together in the previous pages, and it's safe here. Let go. Ask God to clear your mind and help you be honest, especially with yourself. What do you have to lose?

What would you change if you could just snap your fingers and make it happen? Would it be a change in your faith, your life, or your business? What would those areas look like if you could have *each* of them exactly the way you wanted them? Got a picture? Go deeper.

- **IF YOUR FAITH WAS STRONG**, what types of conversations would you be having? Who would you want to be around, and who would want to be around you? Whose faith would be stronger because of your example, your story, and your experience? Your MESSage.

- **IF YOU WERE LIVING YOUR LIFE INSTEAD OF MERELY EXISTING OR SURVIVING**, how long would it take to no longer feel exhausted or behind? What would it feel like to live in the moment, regularly?

IF YOUR WORK/BUSINESS/MINISTRY WAS TRULY IMPACTFUL, SATISFYING, *and* PROFITABLE, what would it be like to have people show up because of your reputation, branding, and MESSage? How would it feel to make more than enough money to live fully and be ridiculously generous?

WHAT WOULD *that kind of life* LOOK LIKE FOR YOU?

How would your life, your family's lives, your clients' lives, and others' lives be better? Imagine the look on their faces right now. With that picture in mind, would it inspire and motivate you to show up differently each day?

What kinds of amazing goals and dreams would you be able to pursue with this as your reality?

Seriously, close your eyes and *feel* what that would be like. Let those emotions wash over you.

WHAT DOES YOUR DREAM LIFE LOOK LIKE? WRITE IT AS IF IT *is* YOUR REALITY TODAY.

If you're not crying yet or at least teary-eyed, I'm not sure you really let go ... really allow yourself to dig deeper. Once you have that powerfully compelling imagery in your mind, I want you to take it a step further. Imagine it's five years from now. You're continuing to take action, reaching your goals, and celebrating those milestones.

How much better is life for you and those around you because of your clarity, focus, and consistency?

Keep going—ten years from now. Where do you live, vacation, and travel? Who do you support, sponsor, or donate to? What have you facilitated, created, or originated through your generosity?

SCREECH!

Now let's imagine *nothing changes* and you continue to struggle with defining who you are beyond those titles, labels, achievements, and your history.

What about your relationship with God and understanding His will for you? If your faith remains what it is today, is it enough to support that envisioned future?

What price are you paying by *not* taking action? Is your fear, doubt, or procrastination what's costing you your relationships, your finances, and maybe even your well-being?

VAL, listen: It's not for lack of *trying.* So many of us are right there with you—frustrated and ready to give up at this very moment because we, too, have *tried* following everything we've been told:

- Religion/Ministry (and how it should not be mixed in the marketplace)
- Time management (your schedule is the "problem"– oh, sister, I've got lots to say about this one in coming chapters)
- Societal must-haves (from the latest technology to the best education)

Well, at the risk of sounding like them … I believe the problem is that you have lost sight of your dream.

IT ALL COMES BACK TO YOUR DREAM

As I said earlier, we all have one common purpose: to share the good news of God's love to others through our Christ-redeemed lives. The purpose may be common, but the execution, *not so much.* God is too big, too creative, and way too fun to have us all doing it the same way!

God gifted you with that dream in your heart because it's meant to be your gift to a specific group of people. We'll talk more about them in a later chapter, but I can tell you now that they've been waiting for you. They need to hear your MESSage. There *is* someone God has been preparing and arming you to stand in the gap for *through* your dream.

Standing in the gap is *part* of our common purpose. It's what I'm hopefully doing right now for you. Think of it as being the guide who extends their hand when crossing over a divide. *You* are someone's guide with a helping hand and a unique perspective and experience for their journey ahead. You picked up this book and you've read this far; you're ready.

I even believe that you are closer than you think to achieving solid faith, a satisfying life, and the strengthened business you've imagined.

Don't miss out on the amazing dream God has given you. The one that you, your family, and your clients deserve to be a part of! And here's the thing, VAL (Valued Amazing Lady—I'll keep saying it 'til you believe it!), until you begin to explore and pursue

SEE, I WILL DO
A NEW THING.
IT WILL BEGIN
HAPPENING NOW.
WILL YOU NOT
KNOW ABOUT IT? I
WILL EVEN MAKE
A ROAD IN THE
WILDERNESS, AND
RIVERS IN THE
DESERT.

- Isaiah 43:19 NLV

that dream of yours, it's going to hang around and nag at you until you do something about it.

EXPLORERS UNITE

Several years ago, I had no idea my childhood love for chalkboards and speaking to a pretend audience was a clue to my future. Or that resisting the idea of legalistic religion would get me fired up enough to speak up. Yet, *God had every intention of using all of this and more* in order to lead me to where I am today: Standing in the gap for women who have forgotten what Valued, Amazing Ladies they truly are. Women who have forgotten the incredible gifts and beautiful MESSage they have to share with a specific group of people who have been praying and waiting for a guide to show up and stand in the gap for them. Know that God has been preparing to send you, too.

I've since traded the chalkboard for flip charts and dry-erase boards and my once imaginary audience has turned into actual audience members, clients, blog readers, social followers, and podcast listeners. I never became a Bible teacher, but I do rely heavily on biblical principles to find truth and encouragement in order to help VALs understand that their dream is not dead; it's exactly what they were destined to pursue. There is no doubt in my mind that my business today is part of growing into what God uniquely designed and created me to do.

If you've ever asked, *"What's the matter?"* or *"What's missing?"* from your life, I hope you feel like you're finally getting somewhere. It's important you understand that your history points to your bigger story. Both the present and the future are tied together in that dream of yours!

DISCOVER

CLOSING THE GAPS IN YOUR GOAL-GETTING

Congratulations! you just finished Part 1 Define, but before we get to what it takes to close the gaps in your goal-getting, I thought this was the perfect spot for a half-chapter.

I'm not sure if half-chapters are a thing, but alas, here we are about to embrace it. Since this is my first go at book writing, I figured it's easier to ask for forgiveness than permission, right? Besides, I didn't know how else to share this important information with you.

The goal is to equip you to better handle and understand what's coming in Chapter 5 and those that follow. They're all about helping you clarify what's needed for your journey ahead.

So please allow me this brief detour, by way of a half-chapter about the most important part of your focus, your brain! And I encourage you to explore each aspect of the next few pages more extensively on your own.

CHAPTER 4.5

The Right D.O.S.E.

A HALF-CHAPTER ABOUT
FINDING YOURS

YOUR BRAIN IS BEAUTIFUL AND AMAZING, AND IS EQUIPPED WITH SPECIFIC CHEMICALS. When any one of these brain chemicals is out of balance, it can cause depression, anxiety, insomnia, memory loss, and digestion issues. Because they're so important, let's explore each one to better understand the roles they play in our mental and physical health.

This is not a comprehensive report or study. It's just my heart to share what I wish had been given to me long ago: a Post-it® note version about the role and function of these brain chemicals: Dopamine, Oxytocin, Serotonin, and Endorphins (D.O.S.E.). Being able to grasp the role and function of each brain chemical is important, but remembering them can be a challenge, hence the acronym.

D.O.S.E.

Discovering the right D.O.S.E. of these natural chemicals can literally be life-changing. I sincerely believe understanding them will tremendously help you to identify what's distracting you or what keeps you pointed in the right direction. Plus, it will be helpful to have this information in mind as we continue through the remainder of this book together.

D IS FOR DOPAMINE.

Just the expectation of achievement releases energy (dopamine), which motivates us to continue to make and pursue goals. Isn't that interesting? The expectation of achievement releases dopamine. No wonder it's known as the "feel-good" chemical. Dopamine → think reward.

O IS FOR OXYTOCIN.

Consciously *building trust* stimulates oxytocin. It's that feeling that someone will protect you. When someone betrays your trust, however, it creates a memory and now a pattern of when to withhold your trust. But you can stimulate that good ol' oxytocin feeling again when you consciously build bonds with those whom you *do* trust. This requires realistic expectations from you and those you choose to trust, so boost your oxytocin by *trusting and verifying that trust.* Then repeat! Oxytocin → think love.

S IS FOR SEROTONIN.

Serotonin not only helps with *mood regulation,* but it also has a key role in other parts of your health including sleep, digestion, bone health, and more. Serotonin affects you psychologically, cognitively, as well as physiologically. Levels that are found to be too high or low can cause what's called Serotonin Syndrome. And yes, it can be very serious. Serotonin → think self-care. (And no, that's not selfish.)

E IS FOR ENDORPHINS.

This chemical *diminishes perceptions of pain*. This "natural pain-killer" can come from a brief euphoria or an emergency. The moments immediately following giving birth would be my personal example of the brief euphoria that masks pain. For others, it may be the absence of pain from an injury or an accident while you are focused on getting help. Less extreme ways to experience endorphins would be when you push past your comfort level. This is common in exercise and known among athletes as a runner's high. Increased boosts of endorphins can come from exercise, overcoming an uncomfortable/stretch goal, or even laughing ('til you're sore). Endorphins → think natural painkiller.

Before you start discovering your right D.O.S.E., here are a few things to keep in mind:

- Overuse of **D**opamine can lead to addiction or impulsive behavior, but too little can lead to depression.
- Too much **O**xytocin can cause social exclusion and negative effects on memory and attention.
- An overabundance of **S**erotonin can lead to depression, anxiety, or worse, Serotonin Syndrome.
- Excessive levels of **E**ndorphins can lead to injury or addiction.

PRIORITIZED FOCUS: CAN YOU THINK OF HEALTHY TRIGGERS THAT WILL ENSURE YOUR PROPER D.O.S.E. OF THESE NATURAL BRAIN CHEMICALS?

DOPAMINE (REWARD)

OXYTOCIN (LOVE)

SEROTONIN (SELF-CARE)

ENDORPHIN (PAIN KILLER)

Got 'em? Good, because not all the natural chemicals in your brain are about your "happiness." (Sigh.)

BUT WAIT, THERE'S MORE. . .

Before we wrap up our mini-chapter on *loosely* defining D.O.S.E. and a quick point of reference for your own D.O.S.E., there's another important chemical worth mentioning: cortisol.

Cortisol is an unhappy chemical in the brain. But it's not necessarily bad because *it's the one that alerts you to pay attention that something may not be in your best interest.*

We know that everything can't always be sunshine and roses, but we can at least put in our due diligence to be better prepared. We are imperfect humans living in a world with other imperfect humans. Bad things are going to happen and sometimes they are going to happen to you.

Cortisol alerts you when your "happy chemicals" take a dip. Some people aren't comfortable letting their D.O.S.E. dip. Instead, they immediately try and mask their cortisol with a D.O.S.E. that they are familiar and comfortable with. Seems harmless enough short-term, but it's definitely harmful in the long run since it can actually increase cortisol levels. Remember, its job is to alert you to potential threats and harm, unlike the happy chemicals, whose job is to point you to the potential reward.

Learn to accept the cortisol dips. That way, you won't rush to mask it with short-term relief that can be potentially harmful in the long term.

And guess what? When you're not trying to squelch your cortisol, you'll end up with more of the D.O.S.E. you want! A good balance of these natural chemicals in your brain is going to greatly affect your happiness (or at least your perception of it).

I CANNOT STRESS THIS PART
ENOUGH: SOME OF US CAN
REGULATE THIS IMBALANCE
NATURALLY WHILE OTHERS
MAY NEED PROFESSIONAL
HELP TO GET BACK IN
BALANCE. NO MATTER IF
THIS IMBALANCE CAME FROM
AN INJURY, OVERWHELMING
CIRCUMSTANCES, OR
SOMETHING ELSE, I
ENCOURAGE YOU TO SEEK
PROFESSIONAL HELP.
ESPECIALLY IF YOU FIND
YOURSELF FEELING HOPELESS
AND HELPLESS AND
HAPPINESS SEEMS LIKE IT'S
JUST UNATTAINABLE TO YOU.

Whether you pause now to check your D.O.S.E. or keep reading, know that I'm proud of you! Yes, that's me over here cheering for you and praying for your ability to carry out what's been entrusted to you. Just know that you're never going to *feel* ready. This is why I felt this half-chapter was such an important prep for the next one. You'll understand why *your* D.O.S.E. is so important and necessary because now we're going to tackle the 4 Frustrating F's.

EXCELLENCE WITHOUT EFFORT IS AS FUTILE AS PROGRESS WITHOUT PREPARATION.

– William Arthur Ward

CHAPTER 5

Those 4 Frustrating F's

NO ONE LIKES FEELING STUCK. We like winning because it's fun. Achieving a goal is satisfying. Making progress is motivating. Feeling stuck when you are trying to win, achieve, or make progress, well, that just stinks!

In this chapter, we are going to cover the four main areas that I believe keep us repeatedly feeling stuck. You know what they say: With knowledge comes power. So, when you combine half-chapter 4.5 and this one, you will be equipped to combat any cycles of stuckness that come up!

A STICKY TRUTH ABOUT STUCK

Feelings are indicators of something bigger that are often related to an unresolved issue or problem. In other words, feelings are symptoms of something else. And here's another fun little tidbit: feelings follow choice. We often identify stuck as a place or a problem in and of itself, but the truth is it's actually a feeling. So when you say that you're stuck, you're actually expressing a feeling that's indicating a bigger, unresolved issue and it's within your control to change.

Feeling stuck is pointing out that something is needed, lacking, or missing. Each of these "somethings" can be (and most likely is) different for all of us, yet we all experience similar symptoms. See if any of these feelings indicate a bigger issue in your own life:

- Unmotivated (possible unresolved issue: lack of purpose)
- Overwhelmed (possible unresolved issue: perfectionism; negative self-image)
- Frustration (possible unresolved issue: lack of progress)
- Depression or anxiousness (possible unresolved issue: proper D.O.S.E.; see Chapter 4.5)

See how sticky this can get?

When you're not making progress toward your goals you feel stuck. Guess what that means? *Stuck is the feeling indicating the bigger issue, the need for growth.* Basically, you are too comfortable in your comfort zone. Yet, what typically happens when you find yourself feeling stuck?

- You complain that "nothing's happening."
- You over-analyze the kabillion reasons why you're "not making progress."
- You keep doing the same things you've been doing but expect different/better results.

Don't you agree feeling stuck is an indicator that maybe you need to grow in a certain area? Think about it: Every time you stretch past your comfort zone, no matter what the goal, what happens?

You grow!

Consider a plant. What's the first thing a seed must do in order to grow? Isolate. It has to get buried in the dirt where it is dark and alone before it can bust out of its shell/casing. Then it has to dig deeper into the soil in order to take root while simultaneously pushing upward, past its familiar and comfy "seed home." With persistence, it keeps pushing up, up, up toward the light.

When it finally breaks the surface, it's small, frail, and seemingly insignificant. As it matures, it continues to push, dig, and grow. Whether it's a tree in a forest or a flower in a field, it becomes part of greater beauty, strength, and purpose, yet can still be recognized for its individuality.

Does any of that sound familiar? Like the seed of your dream that God planted in your heart? The one that you're responsible for protecting and growing so that it, too, can bear fruit? (Chapter 2)

VAL, you Valued, Amazing Lady, you have a choice to make. You can stay feeling stuck inside your seed pod or put in the work to grow into the greater beauty, strength, and purpose you were uniquely designed to achieve through your God-given dream. That dream is His vision for your greater purpose and He's provided all that you need in order to pursue it effectively and productively.

THE 4 FRUSTRATING F'S

Like I said before, life's not all sunshine and roses, so we'll have to do what we can to handle the storms. To that point, there are four

NOW ALL GLORY
TO GOD, WHO IS
ABLE, THROUGH
HIS MIGHTY
POWER AT WORK
WITHIN US, TO
ACCOMPLISH
INFINITELY MORE
THAN WE MIGHT
ASK OR THINK.

- Ephesians 3:20 NLT

main areas in our lives that either keep us stuck or help us grow. I have found these to be among the top causes of our biggest obstacles or catalysts in our best strides toward making progress. A few years ago, I dubbed them *The 4 Frustrating F's.*

Let me give you a quick introduction before we dig into each of one.

Don't get too hung up on their order; just let each area sink in for a minute. I think you'll be in agreement that these areas are indeed frustrating, even overwhelming at times. And depending on their state, they have the ability to make us *feel* stuck!

THE 4 FRUSTRATING F'S

Finances
Are they ever "right" where you want them?

Family/Friendships
Some relationships are better than others ....

Faith
It's what you act on the outside because of what you believe on the inside ... or fake to please or fool others.

Fuel
It's what sparks, drives, and ignites the *you* that is *you.*
It's the thing that brings joy and satisfaction!

Any one of these 4 Frustrating F's can put us on edge, at the edge, or over the edge depending on their state. As in if they're not where we expect or want them to be —would you agree?

What would you say is the state of your 4 Frustrating F's right now? Could they be showing any symptoms of feeling stuck? Are they interrupting or delaying any progress you were making toward your big dream? Use the activity below to help you shed some light on your current situation.

HOW FRUSTRATING ARE EACH OF YOUR F'S RIGHT NOW?

(1 = extremely frustrating to 10 = not frustrating at all because it's right where I want it)

FINANCES

1   2   3   4   5   6   7   8   9   10

FAMILY/FRIENDSHIPS

1   2   3   4   5   6   7   8   9   10

FAITH

1   2   3   4   5   6   7   8   9   10

FUEL

1   2   3   4   5   6   7   8   9   10

Don't worry—I'm not going to just leave you and those questions hanging out there. Let's get to treating those symptoms, VAL.

FRUSTRATING FINANCES

Ever hear the term "financial freedom"? Yes, that was rhetorical; we've *all* heard that phrase before. It's also probably the number-one carrot dangling over many goals and endeavors. We think we understand what it means, but do we really?

Imagine being able to decide where and when to spend your time, in the way that you wanted and with whom you wanted. Well, guess what?

FINANCES ARE THE CURRENCY THAT EITHER PREVENTS YOU FROM THE THINGS YOU WANT OR PROPELS YOU TOWARD THE FREEDOM TO CHOOSE.

It's the catalyst or deterrent for where, when, and how you spend your time and money. So VAL, when it comes to your finances, are they enough to propel you toward what you are trying to achieve?

If they are preventing you from spending where, when, and with who you want, take some time to ponder your next financial move. Be honest in evaluating how much *freedom* your current state of finances is giving you.

What would you have to do in order to *freely choose* how you spend your time and money? You'd probably have to do something uncomfortable.

Maybe something like:

- have a yard sale,
- stop ordering in or going out,
- wait on the new ___ (car, clothes, online course ... yes, even if it's "for" your business), or
- maybe even tell your kids (and yourself), "No, you can't go ... or do ... or have *right now*." (Keywords: "right now." Be sure to catch that.)

Take a moment to think of what it would take for you to move this Frustrating F of finances from a preventative one to a propelling one. In other words, what dollar amount gains you freedom from frustration? (Go ahead; I'll wait.)

PRIORITIZED FOCUS:

Work out your propelling number & brainstorm ideas on how to get there.

I'm willing to guess that your propelling financial number was less than compelling just now. It was most likely conservative because you don't want to seem greedy or you are just uncomfortable thinking big! Is any former religious legalism kicking in, making you feel guilty about money and what it's supposed to be for ... and not?

If you are anything like I was, you probably just tallied up all the bills in your head and added a *little bit more*. Yet, in Chapter 4, we went deep into what your dream a year, five, and even ten years from now could look like. Remember how *big* you went there in your faith, your life, and your business?

Now, with your memory jogged, let's look again. This time, are you able to move past your needs and have the financial freedom mindset to also be a catalyst for someone else's? Think back to the questions and exercise we did about your dream life back in Chapter 4.

How propelling or preventative is that financial number now? Even more than that, how compelled are you to do something to achieve it? Now you know why the space to work it out seemed bigger than necessary. Feel free to go back and work out that financial mindset some more.

But for now, let's leave this financial frustration alone and move on to the next Frustrating F.

FRUSTRATING FAITH

Maybe you're about to skip this part because you're like many who find faith as just a synonym for religion. As in, they are both one and the same. This isn't surprising since the word "faith" often represents what we have been told about it more than we've really seen or experienced. But the reality is that religion is a particular system based on what man believes faith and worship should look like.

For many of us, our own faith is rarely big enough. Since we often feel a sense of being "less than" or behind, this "F" can be quite frustrating. We're pretty good at humble pride, unresolved inferiority complexes, imposter syndromes, or just not stepping into our God-given identity—the usual suspects behind our faith "frustrations" (aka, symptom and bigger issue). Oh, sure we can rattle off a list of names of those who have big faith (most definitely bigger than ours), which only feeds our frustration.

Jesus Himself said that He is the way, the truth, and the life and that no one gets to the Father (God) except through Him (John 14:6). When you seek out a *relationship* with Jesus for yourself instead of an *interpretation of Him through the man-made system of religion,* that is when your faith really grows ... and shows!

Well, would you look at that ... the cure for stuck: growth!

WHEN YOU SEEK OUT
A RELATIONSHIP WITH
JESUS FOR YOURSELF
INSTEAD OF AN
INTERPRETATION OF HIM
THROUGH THE MAN-MADE
SYSTEM OF RELIGION,
THAT IS WHEN YOUR
FAITH REALLY GROWS ...
AND SHOWS!

FAITH = FOUNDATION

Your faith is the foundation of what you believe, which inspires and drives your determination to stand up for that belief. That personalized faith is now the basis for the actions you choose to take in order to live out that belief. *Those actions are the result of your beliefs.*

Wouldn't it make sense to be sure whose truth you are putting your faith into?

Would your faith look different if you verified the answers on your own rather than taking someone else's word for it, whether it came by way of religion, an industry expert, an author, an influencer, a celebrity … or even the book you're reading right now? Yes, my faith in action is the book you're reading right now, but I first had to decide *Who* I was putting my faith into before I could write it!

PROOF FOR YOURSELF

Listen, we are told and sold a lot of "truth" these days. However, as I previously mentioned, I believe that proof is truth and the truth always finds a way to prove itself. It's the number one reason I spend so much time in the Bible. The only truth that I've found to be the most relevant, helpful, realistic, undisputed, and even personal, has come from God's Word. Many of those cool quotes found on social media can be traced back to a verse found in the Bible. Seriously, give the book of Proverbs a good read and you'll find a lot of today's familiar sayings.

How about you? Where does your truth come from, and what evidence do you accept as proof? Do you look for evidence in your own patterns, circumstances, and even the miracles of your life? Yes, I believe in and have experienced miracles. You probably have too, but maybe you're not quite confident enough in your faith to call them that—yet. When your faith is based on truth and continually strengthened, you'll recognize a *lot* more miracles in your life.

I'll share one of mine with you. In April of 2021, I discovered a lump that seemed quite large; probably the size of a golf ball. Hoping I was imagining things, I went to my husband and younger daughter to confirm its existence. Of course, they both urged me to see a doctor. During one of our usual, and bazillion text exchanges with my dear friend and sister in Christ, Monica, I mentioned the concern and that begrudgingly I'm going to have to get it checked out. The next thing I know she's FaceTiming me and as soon as answer the call and see her, she says, "Let's pray!" After instructing me to put my hand directly on this lump on my breast, she asked me, "Do you believe that God can heal you?" I thought that was an odd thing to ask. She knows I believe that God can heal. Yet she persisted: "Do you believe God can heal *you*? Do you believe He has the power, authority, and desire to remove *your* lump?"

At that moment, I realized how much more I believed in miracles for others than what I believed God could do for me. Sure, there were things that I could look back on in my life and see the divine intervention and protection. I could even recognize miracles from another specific and devastating situation from a few years earlier involving my oldest, but that's for another time. This time I was being asked to put *my* faith in action.

When I answered, "Yes," she began to pray healing over my body. Tears rolled down my face as I literally felt the lump shrink to about the size of a small marble. Talk about instantly growing your faith!!

That lump stayed marble size for a few days before eventually going away completely. I believe God did that to solidify my faith and to remind me that there really was a big lump there! It was an undeniable miracle, but I had to believe it was possible first.

We will spend more time on the subject of faith, specifically as it relates to faith in ourselves and the truth we believe about ourselves, but first we have another Frustrating F to address.

FRUSTRATING FUEL

Fuel—the igniter of your soul. If your soul had a face, this would make it smile! It's "that thing" that inspires you and because of it, you become motivated.

Fuel is also the Frustrating F that gets ignored the most. Burnout, and dare I say, feeling stuck in an emotional state of unhappiness is often the result of ignoring this F. (But not if you know your proper D.O.S.E – wink!)

Let's take a little side trip in order to clarify some things when it comes to fuel frustrations. After this little detour, you'll know exactly what I mean by Frustrating Fuel.

PURPOSE VS. PASSION

Raise your hand if you get confused when it comes to differentiating between finding your purpose and following your passion. (I see you.)

When it comes to *pursuing our happiness,* we're often given the advice: find your purpose or follow your passion. Apparently, we are to believe that if we do this, we will not only find happiness but life's successes, too. (Woo-hoo! I'm in! You?)

Hmmm … then why are so many of us still unhappy and not measuring up to our success potential? The short answer is because we've defined them wrong.

You don't find happiness; it's a state of mind (and a D.O.S.E., remember?).

*Success is a journey and a process
that is different for everyone.*

Newsflash! There is no exact formula, but there is one main ingredient, and it's called *work*. The following table outlines what I found when it comes to the differences between purpose and passion and why it's helpful in understanding *your fuel*.

PURPOSE	PASSION
the reason for meaningful work	the result of meaningful work
benefits others	is about YOU (not in a selfish way, it's what energizes you)
has a focused aim	
gives significance	can change (one day you're into painting, the next gardening)
PURPOSE = IMPACT	gives satisfaction
	PASSION = YOUR STYLE BEHIND YOUR IMPACT

Are you gaining some clarity here or is there still some confusion? Maybe you're wondering, *"Can my passion be my purpose?"* Great question! And it seems to be such a popular "success strategy" doesn't it?

Well, here's how I'll sum it up for you and then let you decide: Your purpose is not about your worldly goals (things like career, wealth, or recognition) but about having an impact. Think of your purpose as your impact.

Your passion can be a *vehicle*, but it's not a destination—think of it as the color or personality behind your dreams. Consider your passion as the style behind your impact. Our passions are personal and colorful and they keep us from getting bored and giving up. Our purpose sets us apart from each other, yet always for the benefit of each other.

Okay, that was the end of the mini-trip about passion and purpose, but see how important they were in understanding this particular Frustrating F—Fuel?

YOUR PASSIONS CAN BE USED TO ENERGIZE AND FUEL YOUR PURPOSE.

Take some time to consider your fuel, your purpose, and even your passions. Remember, we all have one common purpose, but in this case, think of purpose as it relates to your specific, unique, God-given dream.

How much more energy do you think you would have if you prioritized the things that fueled you? Consider the things that you no longer make the time to do. Are there any clues pointing to a leaky fuel tank?

For example, maybe you miss painting. What would it take to prioritize the time to paint again? If you miss exercising, how willing are you to prioritize the time to work out? Do you like encouraging others? When and how can you prioritize the time to write and speak that encouragement more? I think you get the picture.

PRIORITIZED FOCUS:

What does it look like to be fueled up in *your* real life?

What fuels you has the power to influence where you are and where you want to be! So if you are less than thrilled with where you are, look no further than your fuel tank.

Now that you have a better understanding of this Frustrating F, you're ready to dig into the final, and probably most complicated, Frustrating F.

FRUSTRATING FRIENDS/FAMILY

This Frustrating F is all about our *relationships*. The ones we have, get to have, have to have, want to keep, need, and maybe even those we … well, you get it.

Do I even have to point out the symptoms of being stuck that are associated with relationships? This Frustrating F is the one that will show how determined you are to *improve or prove* something within those relationships. I've been in more than my share of relationships where proving was more important than improving. Can you guess how those ended up?

It took me years to learn this one incredible lesson about relationships: You can love and forgive a toxic person without needing their presence or permission to do so. (← Someone needs to read that again.)

By the way, some of these people still have access to my inner-circle relationships. (now you don't have to wonder why my "circle" is more dot-like) These people have deeply hurt me *and* those around me. Yet, forgiving them has released the "hold" they had on me and I was able to move on.

Is it easy? No, not really. It requires *regular* divine intervention, prayer, and serious faith in what God has promised. But I can tell you that even when old habits and feelings come up or these toxic people try to "break in" again, I no longer have anxiety about how I'll react to whatever hurtful things they might say or worry about what they'll try to do next. I chose to give up vengeful thoughts, stopped hanging on to hurt feelings, and let go of any unforgiveness a long time ago. *I even found a way to love these individuals.* All people are God's people after all. (Remember I said I believed and experienced miracles? There's another one right there.)

I will warn you by saying this: *Just because you forgive a toxic person, it does not automatically grant them access to you and a pass to be back in your life.* Bless and release from your side of the fence and close that gate!

BOUNDARIES

All relationships need boundaries. We tend to focus on only the toxic or unhealthy relationships needing boundaries, but that's simply not true. All relationships need boundaries.

There was a time when my oldest child really struggled to define her own boundaries. There was some hurt, confusion, and downright betrayal happening with some people. She wanted to put up boundaries but was conflicted because of the relational positions they held.

I walked her through the following exercise in order to help her visualize the importance of boundaries *and* understand that she had the power and right to enforce who "belongs" where. Maybe the same can help you, too.

I instructed her draw a big house with a large yard and a fence all the way around it. The house with its rooms represented her. The yard with a fence represented the space around her property and the safety inside it.

Then I had her name all the people who were in her life – family, friends, work associates, acquaintances, etcetera. Once she had her list, I told her to write their names in the places where she was comfortable with giving them "access." Many names were outside the fence, some in the front yard, a few in the backyard, and one was even *down the street.* She continued to the inside of her house, each room representing a level of trust. Some names were in the kitchen, others in the living room, and a few in the basement. This exercise gave her a better understanding of what boundaries really look like and the confidence to enforce them. Maybe it just helped you to put some boundaries around your Frustrating Family/Friends, too.

Not sure where to start? Well, think vertically before horizontally. If you focus on looking *up,* He'll show you who belongs beside you, around you, and even behind you! If God can work relational miracles in and for me, He can for you, too!

PRIORITIZED FOCUS:
What will your boundaries look like?

PUTTING IT ALL TOGETHER

Are there frustrating indicators in your finances, faith, fuel, or those family/friends that you are ignoring right now? Don't ignore them; they are pointing to the symptoms that are keeping you feeling stuck! Recognize them for what they really are—something you need, lack, or are missing. In other words: growth.

Growing past your comfort zone is never easy, but always worth it! The thing about getting unstuck is to *do something*. Start small, one step at a time.

The reason so many of us find ourselves continually feeling stuck is that we focus too much on the *"big* end goal" instead of the next small step.

Where would each of your 4 Frustrating F's be if you focused on *the next small step?* Now, what if you were to continually and repeatedly take small steps? I'm sure you would move past feeling stuck and begin to see some actual growth!

LITTLE PRACTICE, BIG IMPROVEMENTS

What if you committed to making *one improvement* to each of the Frustrating F's every month for a year? Nothing drastic or crazy, just a slight tweak, or a nudge past the comfort zone toward growth. Every thirty days you would build on your improvement from the previous month. Imagine what progress you'd make if you practiced this consistently!

Take a moment to brainstorm just a few improvements you could make in each of the frustrating areas for the next few months. Keep them realistic, but also a bit of a stretch.

PICK YOUR F	MONTH 1	MONTH 2	MONTH 3
FINANCES			
FAITH			
FUEL			
FAMILY/ FRIENDS			

You are doing *great*! I am so proud of you. In the next chapter, I'm going to walk you through just *how* to choose your priorities. The right priority, at the right time, and for the right reason. What do you say—are you ready to turn the page?

CHAPTER 6

Choosing Your Priorities

I'M CALLING FOUL ON TIME MANAGEMENT. For years you've been trained and even ingrained to believe that most, if not all, of your goal-getting issues stem from the ability, or lack of, "managing" your time.

It's the number one issue that we love to blame and claim as "the problem" when it comes to falling short of our goals. No wonder this is the case since companies spend millions making sure that you are being told and sold that it's your number one goal-getting roadblock. You're told about scheduling must-haves and dos, then sold the latest products and protocols to solve your time-management issues. Time management is even being told and sold to you as a goal itself!

Time management is not *the* problem or even *your* problem when it comes to your lackluster goal-getting.

You cannot control time, only what you choose to do with it.

QUALITY IS NEVER
AN ACCIDENT.
IT IS ALWAYS
THE RESULT OF
INTELLIGENT
EFFORT. THERE
MUST BE A WILL
TO PRODUCE A
SUPERIOR THING.

– John Ruskin

I can understand the concept behind the term "time management," but it's really misleading, which is why it is so misunderstood *and* misused by so many.

Allow me to share two important facts with you. They may just be the clarity you need to understand this elusive yet oh-so-desired goal known as time management.

IT TAKES TWO

Did you know that time management is actually a skill? To connect this thought, let's look at what a skill even is. *Merriam-Webster* defines a skill as "the ability to use information effectively so that you can execute or perform a task." Skills are something that can be learned and even improved with practice. In other words, skill takes *work*.

That could be a first clue as to why this time-management thing is so elusive. It's revered and desired by many, but achieved by few. Why? Because it's a skill, something that takes information *combined with effort and repeated practice.*

We all want to be part of the time-management elite club, but we treat it as if it's a product you can just grab off the shelf. By now you know it's just not that easy. Time management is a skill that belongs to those who put in the work and repeatedly practice to improve it.

Listen, I'm not here to discourage you from becoming a member of the time-management elite club. I'm right there with ya! But I do want us to be better informed and equipped as to what it's going to take to get there. Once we understand these facts and what we need to do, it becomes a whole new ball game.

Now that you have this important insight into what time management is and requires of us, let's take it a step further. After all, our goal is to be among the few that master this skill, right?

Before you jump to evaluating your time-management skills, let's look at fact number two: methods. The very next thing that needs our attention, understanding, and implementation are methods or systems in order to *showcase* our time-management skills. Methods can be invented, changed, and even personalized. Skills, remember, are pieces of information turned into practice that improves a specific task and achieves the desired result. Skills take lots of practice to master.

Methods or systems are the personalized way that you implement those skills for a specific reason. Skills take practice; methods require purpose.

That's where we get all mixed up and messed up, my friend.

There are thousands of methods available to us to help solve our time-management "issues," but very few emphasize the skill necessary to effectively execute them. So what's a VAL to do?

WE CONSISTENTLY BUY THE METHODS WITHOUT FACTORING IN THE SKILL NEEDED TO UTILIZE THEM.

THE WILL TO PRACTICE AND IMPLEMENT

In later chapters, I'm going to share an effective innovation that I call the Prioritized F.O.C.U.S. method. I'll share three versions: a F.O.C.U.S. method for faith, one for everyday life, and the other for business goals. It is a method I have utilized, taught, and tweaked over the years with great success and effectiveness.

However, without the knowledge of how to apply that information by identifying skills that can be practiced, the method is much less effective. Skills and methods go hand in hand.

And I will note that just because it's "my method," it doesn't mean that you need to do it "my way." I actually encourage you to take the information and tweak it to how and where it makes sense in *your* situation. That way, you will not only come up with your own *method*, but a *system* that works!

Think of your skills as tools and your methods as weapons in the battle for your priorities.

Using a dull ax requires great strength, so sharpen the blade. That's the value of wisdom; it helps you succeed.

- ECCLESIASTES 10:10 NLT

Now before you skip ahead to the F.O.C.U.S. methods, there's still a bit more information we need to cover—and not just information for you to hoard and never use, but information that you need to take in and apply.

That's wisdom VAL, and now's the time we put the "B" in front of our "older" status. In addition to being older and wiser, it's time to be BOLDER! Boldness is the only way to get from "you are here" to there—your desired destination.

CHA-CHA THROUGH IT, VAL!

Ahh, if only it were that easy! Believe me when I tell you this—learn to love the cha-cha! You know, the dance that takes you one step forward, two steps back …. That's what it's going to feel like as you work on getting ahold of your priorities. But at least the cha-cha is fun, right?

There's still plenty of work to be done *and repeated*. See, that's the part that trips a lot of us up. Why? Well, what happens when you repeat the same things over and over again without success? You tend to either believe that you "aren't able to learn your lesson" or you get bored and decide to go find something more exciting.

But, on the flip side of the coin, think about your most successful patterns. You became successful because you repeated certain actions! If it ain't broke ….

This is how we need to look at creating a system that moves us toward our goals. We need to choose to learn the right skills and then plug them into the right methods.

FOCUS CHECK

By now, you should have defined and prayerfully clarified these areas:

* Your core values—who you *really* are beyond titles, achievements, and labels.
* Your dream—who it's from, why it's been entrusted to you, and its connection to your MESSage.
* Your "right" D.O.S.E.
* The Frustrating F's that can keep you feeling stuck if you don't address the real issue.
* The skills you need to improve in order to achieve better time management.

Reviewing where we've been is important to help us retain the information so that it can begin to be applied. These are the building blocks of a necessary process.

You can have a beautiful house on the outside, but without a strong foundation holding it up, it won't stay pretty for long!

BREATHE EASIER

Look at this process as the much-needed CPR to your dream. By now I would hope that we've established that your dream is *not* dead. Besides, there's a big difference between mostly dead and all dead (remember *The Princess Bride* and Miracle Max?). The truth is that your dream probably just needs a bit of life breathed back into it.

Thankfully, if you've read this far you should be feeling a little more oxygen flowing back to your dream by way of some CPR, which, as you may recall from this book's Introduction, stands for Core values, Prioritization, and Resources.

As we saw in the previous section, the "C" in the CPR for your dream often represents more than just the *core* of your values, but also the *clarity* you need to grow past any *comfort* zones!

Now we're going to dig into the "P," which is all about knowing when, where, and how to work toward that dream of yours through *intent focus.* You will literally be able to prioritize your focus on the right thing at the right time. Plus, you'll be confident in knowing that it's for the right reason.

SKIP THE OVERWHELM AND S.O.S.

As you think of your big dream, I'm willing to bet you are already starting to feel overwhelmed with ideas, options, and some decisions. Maybe even to the point of indecision.

If so, stop and take a breath. The last thing you need right now is to be sabotaged by that sneaky S.O.S. (Shiny Object Syndrome)! I'm willing to bet that 9.5 out of 10 of us suffer from S.O.S. on a daily basis.

And it's no wonder. From the moment we turn on our devices— the TV, our phone, computer, or even the radio (yes, some of us still listen to that)—we are hit with ads for things to consider trying or buying. Which one do you choose to listen to, follow, or buy? Every choice can be the right one ... or the wrong one!

IF SOMETHING
PROMISES TO
TAKE YOU FROM
BROKE, BUSTED,
AND DISGUSTED IN
WHAT SEEMS LIKE
AN UNREASONABLY
SHORT AMOUNT
OF TIME - PAUSE,
PONDER, AND PRAY.

Alternatively, maybe you've gathered momentum from pumping some CPR back into your dream and the options seem *urgent*. Again, stop and take a breath. If something promises to take you from broke, busted, and disgusted in what seems like an unreasonably short amount of time, you need to pause, ponder, and pray. Otherwise, you may find yourself inspired to see how far you can push your bank account and relationships. Beware when those types of distractions flash before your eyes, ears, and inbox.

PAUSE, PONDER & PRAY

4 things to consider if you find yourself suffering from S.O.S:

1. IS IT ONE OF YOUR TOP 3 PRIORITIES IN YOUR LIFE RIGHT NOW?

Have a list of priorities for this season in your life—not sure? We'll get to that in a moment.

2. IS IT A DISTRACTION IN DISGUISE?

This simply means that it's sort of where you want to go, but it should really go in the "file" for later when you're actually ready for it.

3. DOES THE OFFER OR THE PERSON SHARE YOUR VALUES?

For example, you value God and family first and foremost; do they?

4. IS IT SOMETHING YOU CAN APPLY TO YOUR LIFE RIGHT NOW?

Or do you need to have xyz in place first, a certain amount of money set aside, a lot of time to dedicate to it, etc.

I have found three keys that can unlock your prioritized focus, *even in the midst of the ever-increasing S.O.S. moments and endless distractions.* You're going to love these! Use them whenever you feel S.O.S. or another distraction attempting to weasel its way in front of your goal.

3 KEYS TO YOUR PRIORITIZED FOCUS

KEY FOCUS #1
Discover & Understand Your SEASON

There may be four seasons in a year and many in our lifetime, but when it comes to goal getting, there are only three seasons: research, ramp-up, and recovery.

If you ever hope to move beyond a dreamy goal-setter to a consistent goal-getter, you'll need to recognize and navigate these three seasons.

Taking the time to discover and understand the season you're in is a huge contributor to your goal's progress, whether they are the really big ones or the smaller everyday ones you are hoping to achieve.

Pursuing your big dream and the smaller goals it will take to get there requires Prioritized Focus. *So please, before you buy the next pretty planner, mark your calendar, or post on social media about your next BIG goal, consider the season you're actually in right now.*

Let's take a look at these three seasons a bit more closely.

Research Season

You are in a research season if you have acknowledged that your life is legitimately CrAzY busy right now. You had a baby, sent a kid to college, got married, got divorced, lost a loved one, changed jobs, quit your job … you know, big transition things that need you to take a minute. But you still have serious ambitions in the midst of your already important responsibilities.

In this season, you recognize that you can wisely use pockets of time by doing research. Not just any research, but research that pertains specifically to your next goal; the one that you want to see come to fruition in the next 12–18 months. That goal.

If your next goal doesn't seem realistic for the next 12–18 months, that's okay. It doesn't mean that it's not a good or feasible goal (we're going to talk about feasible goals in Chapter 11, but hang with me here). It just means the goal needs to be moved to a further date. One year, three, or five? That's up to you, but you'd be surprised how much *guilt and overwhelm is released when you just assign it a future date.* (Remember, the "R" in CPR is for resources, but I also like to think of it as permission to release the guilt!)

Most of the women that I work with (even those that I don't), attribute overwhelm as their number one obstacle … and the one they have the hardest time overcoming. So be sure to let it go, for now, and assign it a future re-visit date. Keep in mind that God is prepping you for what He has already prepared *for you* so just stay the course.

By the way, if you do not have a timestamp on your goal, it's a daydream, not a goal. Yes, we all have multiple goals and even projects, but without an actual timeframe, it's neither.

A research season can last a few days, weeks, or months depending on your situation and where it falls within your 12–18 month goal. Make no mistake, it's an incredibly valuable season. It's about doing the research now so that you are prepared for the next season. Imagine stepping into the next phase of your goal-getting with all of the research that you can think of already done, listed, and ready to go!

Ramp-Up Season

Ramp-up season is when you now have the time and energy to utilize the research you acquired! *This is the time for massive, intentional action.*

Earlier in this chapter we learned that time management is a skill, and this is where that skill (or lack of it) comes into play. It is crucial for this time period to be planned ahead of time and fiercely protected.

The Ramp-Up Season has the potential to be one of the most prosperous times in your life. Unfortunately, many are unable to realize its full potential because it's not planned for or protected properly.

It takes serious and advanced consideration for the anticipated beginning *and end of this phase*. It's important to take the time to craft a well-thought-out plan and strategy (I'll share the differences between these two in the very next chapter—you're welcome) so you don't find yourself feeling stuck this season.

Recovery Season

This is the stretch that so many goal-getters neglect to take seriously if they consider it at all. All their focus, energies, and efforts are put on the do, to-do, get-it-done, and next lists until they literally have nothing left to give. No gas in the tank, no creativity, no more resources to draw from, and, worst of all, for some, no hand left to grab hold of.

Maybe the failure came from being unwilling to be honest about the reality of the current season, and choosing instead to jump too quickly and eagerly into the one *that was wanted instead of needed*.

How many times have you neglected to recognize the season you're in and didn't do the proper research because you were so anxious to just ramp-up? I know I have. Even as I write this, I can think of times when I was so excited by the *idea* of something that my research season lasted about as long as a Google search result. Can you guess what the actual result was? A ramp-up season so long that everyone was tired of hearing about the idea/goal I had—including me! (Don't let that be you, VAL.)

Too many of us find ourselves in an unexpected recovery season instead of an intentional, celebratory, and restful recovery season. (← Read that again, VAL.)

Broke, busted, and disgusted would be the result of my own unexpected or unplanned recovery seasons.

Alternatively, recovery doesn't have to be unexpected or unwelcome. Celebrating the success of any ramp-up seasons with my family through one-on-one dates that include lingering conversations in fun places would be my example of a celebratory recovery season.

How about you? Take a minute to envision what your recovery seasons could look like (both the sunny planned for and the not-so-sunny unplanned ones).

WRITE THEM DOWN:

Imagine if you took into account the season you are in *before, during, and after* a big goal how much more you could be shouting "Ta-Da!" instead of puffing, "Just one more to-do, just one more" like the Little Engine that Could.

The first key to prioritizing your focus on the right thing at the right time is to discover and understand your seasons.

Think of what you could accomplish if you intentionally planned out your research, ramp-up, and recovery seasons for each goal and project. As a matter of fact, I challenge you to do just that!

*IDENTIFY THE SEASON YOU ARE IN RIGHT NOW:

How do you know?

Based on your next 12–18-month goal, how long do you anticipate this season will last?

KEY FOCUS #2
Discover & Understand Your REASON

When it comes to goal setting, we can get pretty good at justifying a reason to *just go for it*. Some of those reasons may be the result of impulsive S.O.S. moments (just me?), but when it's time to get serious, like really serious, we must have a solid strategy in place.

Here are three questions to ask yourself when you want to get to the root of the REASON for this current goal:

1. Why does this goal even matter to me right now?
2. Who will benefit if I follow through and achieve this goal?
3. What have I already tried before that worked (or didn't) as it relates to this particular type of goal?

We'll go over each of these so that you can discover the answer for each for yourself. Remember, information is one thing, applying it is another, and doing both leads to wisdom!

#1 Why Does It Matter?
The first question is somewhat the easy one because you've already decided in some way that "now's the time" to pursue this goal/project ... but why? This is the question that has you channeling your inner preschooler; you know, the one always asking, "But *why?*"

The more time you dig into answering this question, the better clarity you'll have. Guess what clarity gives you? Direction!

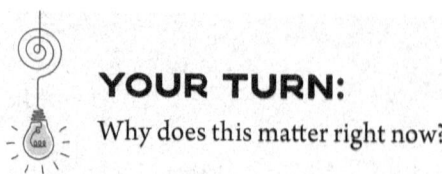

YOUR TURN:

Why does this matter right now?

#2 Who Will Benefit?

The next question puts a little more skin in the game. Who will benefit if you follow through and actually achieve this goal?

When your goals involve others and are for their benefit, you tend to bring a different level of yourself to the table. Awareness that people are watching or counting on you makes you weigh the cost and outcome a little differently.

This question will make you think about moving forward or retreating. Either way, your honest answer will save you time (and maybe even feelings) in the long run.

YOUR TURN:

Who will benefit if you achieve this goal? (Draw from your core value work in Chapter 3 if you need a little more direction or clarity.)

#3 What's Working?

The final question brings into play your level of seriousness and commitment. Things are getting real, VAL. Identifying what you have already tried that worked (or didn't) not only gives you an excellent starting point, but also prompts you to persevere.

How can you improve what you have already tried? What new actions can you take? Listen, everything works great in theory, on paper, and even in our heads. But it's the doing that brings us closer to the actual solutions and destinations. (Ouch!)

YOUR TURN:

When it comes to your current goal's progress—
what's working? What's not working?

Do you feel as though I'm picking on you? Ready to skip ahead to the F.O.C.U.S. methods in the chapters ahead? I get it, I really do. But know that the content was first experienced and applied by me—the tough love and all!

This book is a neatly organized compilation of years' worth of my sticky notes, tears, perseverance, and important lessons. I'm sharing from my experiences and heart with hindsight and practice to help *you* achieve your dream faster and easier. So stick with me, you're doing great!!

Before we move on to what's next, let's be sure that you have a grasp on the first two key areas of focus in order to be a true goal-getter, not just a proficient goal-setter.

KEY FOCUS #3
Discover & Understand What's TEASIN' You

We already covered a big part of what often teases you away from your goals: that pesky Shiny Object Syndrome (S.O.S.), But this step is more about you taking ownership of those syndromes and teasers. The final key to becoming a prioritized focus goal-getter is about responsibility: yours.

Blame shifting is easy and practically second nature, especially when it comes to pinpointing why we aren't where we want to be or thought we'd be "by now." I could easily fill up pages with reasons why I'm not where I should be by now. You?

My excuses typically fall into one of the Frustrating F's (Faith, Family/Friends, Finances, Fuel), some of which could even be my own fault. How about you? Can you list and categorize your shoulda, woulda, and coulda's within the 4 Frustrating F's, too?

While you can't control the things that happen around you or even how others treat you, you can control your responses. (I felt that eye roll! Stick with me.)

When it comes to making progress toward pursuing that God-given dream of yours, it's up to you to decide how serious you're willing to get.

This key of knowing what's teasin' you may sound funny and maybe even a bit silly, but not if you're serious about stepping into the dream God has assigned you.

When it comes to what's teasin' you away from your goal, ask yourself, "What people, places, or things are my go-to when I want to hide or procrastinate?" And then be honest.

Teasin' People

They could be who you interact with in person (cashiers, baristas, servers, co-workers) and those that you are connected to, like family and friends. They could also be strangers, like the people we keep up with on our screens; you know, influencers, celebrities, famous personalities, etcetera.

It's not just about a physical person walking up and disrupting your focus (which is a real thing that happens often); we're going even deeper. I'm asking you to recognize and identify those individuals who are your teaser people *by choice*. You know, the ones that serve as your favorite procrastination hiding spots.

YOUR TURN:

Who are your top teasin' people:

Where can your go-to teasin' people be found? (*Are you hitting them up by text, online search, scroll?*)

Teasin' Places

Do your moods dictate where you can be found? Under the covers, at a table with a beverage, on a couch with snacks, and a binge record to beat. Maybe it's a cart full of retail therapy.

Whether it's hobbies, work, or something else, you need to be aware of what you allow to tease you away from your planned prioritized focus.

We all get the same 24 hours a day to work with. If you want to make the most of yours, take responsibility and ownership of the parts within your control.

YOUR TURN:

Where are your top teasin' places?

How often are you "visiting" these places?

Teasin' Things

I almost skipped this one because it seems so obvious to me that I didn't think it needed an explanation. Then I thought, "is it really obvious to everyone?"

When I think of the things that tease me away from my should-be-doing goals, a few usual suspects come to mind: Checking my social media, email, and weather ... from either my phone, tablet, or desktop. Grabbing another cup of tea. Remembering I didn't put eyeliner on. Deciding that I'm kinda hungry ....

So while teasin' things might seem obvious, see how some sneaky ones get in there?

YOUR TURN:

What are your teasin' things?

How often are you hunting them down?

3 KEYS RECAP

Now you're ready to put it all together. Keep these 3 keys in mind when it comes to your priorities and your day-to-day distractions. They really are key to keeping you focused. But that's a goal in itself!

1. **DISCOVER & UNDERSTAND YOUR SEASON**

   research, ramp-up, or recovery

2. **DISCOVER & UNDERSTAND YOUR REASON**

   Why does this goal even matter to me right now?

   Who will benefit if I follow through and achieve this goal?

   What have I already tried before that worked (or didn't) as it relates to this goal?

3. **DISCOVER & UNDERSTAND WHAT'S TEASIN' YOU**

   people, places, and things

JIGGLE THE HANDLE AND GREASE THAT LOCK

These 3 Keys to Prioritized Focus are not always easy. Sometimes you have to jiggle the lock while turning the handle, or even grease the lock. Meaning, it's not a once-and-done simple solution; it takes work and practice. And remember what work and practice bring? *Skill!*

I've come to find that these 3 keys are among the best tools to have on hand, especially when the goal is to make the most of my time.

Whew! Now that you're also equipped with these 3 keys, I hope that you will use them to filter which of the Frustrating F's needs your prioritized focus the most *in* this season. (See what I did there?)

Imagine what each of those four frustrating areas could look like in a year. You could make one a focused priority, one quarter at a time! Then move on to the next while maintaining the improvements you've made from the last. Rinse and repeat ... every year.

FROM FLUNKY TO FOCUSED

I hope this chapter has helped you understand that *you are not a time management flunky*! Just "under-told" when it comes to the skills needed to implement the methods you've been sold.

Let's agree to be excellent stewards of → Prioritized Focus ←! Stewardship is about being responsible and carefully overseeing and protecting something considered worth preserving.

Stewardship is about being responsible and carefully overseeing and protecting something considered worth preserving.

Now it's time to debunk another popular mix-up: plans and strategies.

IF YOU DIDN'T GET
WHAT YOU WANT,
IT'S EITHER A SIGN
THAT YOU DID NOT
SERIOUSLY WANT
IT, OR THAT YOU
TRIED TO BARGAIN
OVER THE PRICE.

- *Rudyard Kipling*

CHAPTER 7

A Plan Is Not a Strategy

BUT YOU SURE NEED ONE TO ACHIEVE YOUR GOALS!

I'M NOT FLUFFING IT UP. In case you haven't noticed by now, I can be known to deliver a *lot* of information, which can be a bit of an overload for some. Okay, for most, actually.

I could try and impress you with cool stories or funny anecdotes, but that's really just not my style. If I find something that is helpful, relevant, *and* can increase the speed of your goal-getting progress toward your God-given dream, why waste time fluffing it up?

I hope you're in agreement 'cause we're about to untangle a few other common mix-ups. We've already covered: skills + methods, purpose + passion, and your seasons, but there's more. Ones that go beyond defining differences. This chapter will help you discover what's actually effective when it comes to your defined time, priorities, and focus.

PLANNERS, PLANNERS, PLANNERS!

Can I assume that you consider *finding* the planner more fun than the plans themselves? I get it. With all the types of planners, their methods, and so many different styles available, how could one resist the unspoken challenge to try them all? There are planners to fit any lifestyle and every personality.

And let's not forget all of the accessories to go along with the perfect planner: magnets, stickers, special pens, and colored markers. Even wall calendars want in on this planning action. Do you prefer paper or the dry-erase kind? I have both. My dry-erase version has a four-month view, thank you very much. Clearly, I'm not much of a digital gal, but sheesh! There are just as many choices for those!

So with all of those options and choices, who wouldn't get all caught up in the fun of finding your perfect planner and its "necessary" tools? I know that I did.

Before I designed the 30-Day Prioritized Focus Success Planner, I had quite the Goldilocks planner phase. The one where I would go and buy a *new* planner every time I was no longer "inspired" by the current one I was using. Apparently, there was mysterious motivational magic just in the planner aisle. Who knew?!

True story—I'd find myself in a planning aisle about every 8–12 weeks, staring at a shelf full of all my planning needs. I'd tell myself, "Maybe this cover, design, sticker, or pen will make all the difference this time," while thumbing through pages and contemplating which cover sparked the most motivation at that moment.

Eventually, I became frustrated with myself because I could barely stay focused "on my plans" for more than a few weeks at a time, let alone lug them around for an entire year! (No matter how pretty or inspiring their covers were that housed "my plans.") That, VAL, is a super brief history of how the *30-Day Prioritized Focus Success Planner* came to be.

We are captivated by covers, overjoyed with thoughts of organized time, gush over our goals, and the promise of productivity is a pull that we just can't seem to resist. But here's the thing when it comes to our plans, planning, and even the places we put them— we neglect to account for what it actually takes to *execute* those plans.

More often than not, we are excellent initiators of a plan. Executors? Not so much. As soon as "our plan" gets interrupted, life gets a little wonky, or we get bored, it's time for a new plan(ner)!

Later I'm going to help you better prepare for the unexpected *and* the unplanned, but for now, we've got to get "the plan" right— *your plan,* especially what that plan looks like and impacts real life—*your* real life!

WHAT'S THE DIFFERENCE?

The first step in getting your plan right is to understand that there is a distinct difference between a plan and a strategy. Maybe you are already aware of this, but if not, we're about to get it straight right now. *A plan is what you need* in order to move forward toward your goal.

IT'S FASCINATING THAT MOST PEOPLE PLAN FOR A VACATION WITH BETTER CARE THAN THEY PLAN THEIR LIVES. PERHAPS THAT IS BECAUSE ESCAPE IS EASIER THAN CHANGE.

—Jim Rohn

Think of a plan as an inventory of what's needed. Plans answer important questions about your goals like who, what, and why. *You* are already the number-one responsible party, but who else can help? What types of things, resources, tools, and skills will you *need* to make progress toward this goal? We'll dig more into methods soon, but just know for now—you need a plan!

Okay, so we've established that a plan is about what your goal needs; now it's time to clarify it's often missed and neglected partner: strategy. Planning and strategy have become somewhat known as frenemies (likely because one is easier and, dare I say, more fun than the other).

Consider if you agree with this statement: A strategy is the application and execution of your plans, whereas a plan is an inventory of the who, the what, and the why of your goal's needs. Strategy is the *measurable activities* that cover the how, where, and when to execute those defined needs.

Before you move on, be sure you understand the distinction between a plan and a strategy. If you need to re-read and digest the differences between the two, I totally get it, especially if you have never heard of—or thought about—the distinction between the two before.

In an effort to really summarize and pare it down, here's a Post-it Note version of those explanations. Hey, whatever it takes, right?

POST-IT NOTE® VERSION

PLAN = the big picture and the outline of what's needed. The who, the what, and why of your goal's needs.

STRATEGY = the blueprint and the measurable activities for what's needed.

The how, where, and when to attain your goal.

BONUS TERMS

Goal = a singular, targeted direction (future-focused); the desired result

Milestones = the measurable progress made; accomplishments

Method = the repeatable process to achieve goals

THAT WAS EASY

I can practically hear you say, "Oh, well, that clears things up; I'm golden now. Thanks, Deana!"

I think it's safe to presume that by this far in our journey together, you recognize it's *not* that easy. Why else would I dedicate a whole chapter to this particular mix-up and these frenemies? Smart, savvy, and sassy, that's my VAL! *(You Valued, Amazing Lady, you!)* And you're right! I want to make sure that you are clear about the differences and now we're going to shift into how to *keep* it clear.

KEEPING IT CLEAR

We've built quite a foundation so far, but now it's time to dig even deeper. When it comes to mapping out the plan for your current in-front-of-you goal, there are a series of questions you should ask yourself.

These questions are especially important for improving those 4 Frustrating F's we covered back in Chapter 5 and helping you master the 3 Keys to Prioritized Focus from the last chapter. Most importantly, though, is that they'll help you discover your commitment level when it comes to protecting those priorities. The last thing you want is to end up recycling the same unwanted results and excuses that bring you back to feeling broken, busted, and disgusted.

Let's address your plan first. Yes, we talked about what a plan is, but now it's time to discover what that looks like specifically for *you*.

DISCOVERING YOUR P.L.A.N.

There's something that you should know before we go further. In case you haven't already figured it out on your own, I genuinely love acronyms. I use them a lot. Just peruse my website, or look over any of the workbooks that go along with my teachings and pieces of training, and you'll see a bunch of acronyms. I think the reason is because it's the simplest way I've found to remember important definitions and terms so that they can actually be usefully applied.

Meet your P.L.A.N. and get ready to learn how to craft it so it works *for* you. Having a P.L.A.N. will help you make much greater progress than you ever have before when dealing with the state of your 4 Frustrating F's, which goals to work on, and how to prioritize them. Sounds great, right? Well, let's get to it!

PURPOSE

The P in your **P**.L.A.N. is for *Purpose* and it's where you begin. What is the purpose of your goal?

Note that you should always be able to trace the goal to one of the Frustrating F's and identify the season you're in. Then you're better equipped to answer the purpose question.

You're probably feeling like I'm taking you in circles right now. That's understandable since we've talked about purpose before. Think of it this way: Your dream is at the core of a big, messy ball of string. Right now, we are slowly and methodically untangling that string, looking to assess the lengths that we have to work with and what condition they are in before we proceed. Then we can put those pieces in the right place, where they are most useful so that they'll be most effective.

Your dream is really God's vision of what He wants to do *through you* with your time here on earth. The process (the untangling of the string) is His way of molding you into who you need to be in order to handle the job (living your dream).

Have you ever seen the backside of a tapestry? It's a hot mess! But the front, the part that people can see? Stunningly beautiful and a detailed masterpiece! That tapestry is a lot like you and me. We want people to only see and know about that "front part," the Insta-worthy side. We prefer to restrict access to the "back part," the framework that ties *all* the areas of our lives together—the good, bad, pretty, and ugly parts.

ALL THOSE MESSY PIECES
OF OUR LIVES ARE SOMEHOW
WONDERFULLY INTERWOVEN
TOGETHER FOR A SPECIFIC
PURPOSE BY THE MASTER.
WE ARE HIS BEAUTIFUL
MESSTERPIECES!

Think of what you've learned so far as it relates to the word "purpose" and how it serves as the first part of your **P**.L.A.N. Valued, Amazing Lady, so far, you've learned how your core values are the best way to filter decisions and that God has been prepping you for what He has planned for you.

Do you remember the difference between purpose and passion? Quick recap: Purpose has to do with impact and passion about your personal style in how you make that impact. With all of that fresh in your mind, start thinking about how you can begin putting that knowledge into action.

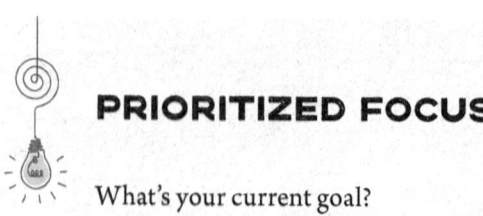

PRIORITIZED FOCUS

What's your current goal?

What's the purpose of this goal?

THINK:

This goal impacts (season, people, reach):

because:

LENGTH

We already busted the myth of time management and saw just how slippery that slope can get until you trade managing for prioritizing. But you dug in and now understand how trading the perspective from trying to manage time to prioritizing it is a much better focus.

So the L in our P.**L**.A.N. is for the *length of time* we allot to our goal(s). And just like our lesson in time management, this can get a bit tricky, too.

The reason it gets tricky is that we typically over or underestimate the time needed to complete any given task. Listen, I've been "writing" this book for about two years, but it wasn't until I started to P.L.A.N. that things actually got moving.

Obviously, the length of time varies, but this is a call to be realistic. Get serious and find the *harmony* between disciplining yourself and extending yourself some grace. Note that I used the word harmony, I like this so much better than the commonly used and expected word, balance. Harmony makes me think of what's peaceful and doable, while balance drums up feelings of overwhelm and unrealistic expectations. Try swapping the words for yourself and see how it feels.

Consider if your goal will take a couple of days, a few weeks, or several months. We are going to be talking about methods soon, so don't get too hung up on the how right now. Just focus on *what results you want.*

Believe it or not, most goals can be achieved in about 30–90 days. Yes, I said *days.* Of course, that will take some serious Prioritized Focus, but don't worry; by the time we're done, you'll have it!

Oh, and it's fair to note that when it comes to *real* change, like creating lasting habits or writing a book, they can typically be achieved in 12–18 months. That should help you establish a realistic eye on not only your goal but your willingness to commit to it as well.

PRIORITIZED FOCUS

Am I being realistic about the length of time I'm giving to this goal? Yes or No

PLACE A CHECKMARK BESIDE THE DURATION THAT'S MOST REALISTIC FOR YOUR CURRENT GOAL:

This goal can be a 30–90-day achievement.

This goal needs to be a 12–18 -month achievement.

GET AS SPECIFIC AS YOU CAN BASED ON WHAT YOU UNDERSTAND SO FAR:

This goal should take me _____ to achieve.

I believe that is a realistic length of time because:

ATTITUDE

How far would you like to delve into the topic of attitude? Well, if you really want to put the "b" in older to become bolder in your dreams and goals, you'll need the "A" in our P.L.**A**.N., which is attitude.

It's commonly said that mindset is 90 percent of both our problem and solution, yet we give it less than 10 percent of our attention.

Are you among those who believe that mindset and attitude are the same things? Well, they're actually *not* the same. Here we go again; one of those common mix-ups.

Your mindset has to do with how you see the world whereas your attitude is how you deal with it. I guess now we know why there's the saying, "Attitude is everything."

Take a moment and think about where you're currently at on this journey and where you desire to go. How's your attitude about it? What's driving those thoughts—your choices or your feelings? Ooh, that's a loaded question right there.

Feelings follow choice, not the other way around. Choices can indicate feelings, but not dictate them.

Being mindful of your mindset is the big takeaway here, followed by your attitude about it! Consider what you think about because you act on what you believe. (Whew! I need that on a Post-it Note'.) Be sure you are feeding your mind with what you want to show up in your life because your brain protects what's familiar. The more you think about your dream, your priorities, and how you'll get there, *the harder your brain will work to protect them.*

PRIORITIZED FOCUS

Do you agree with the following statement?
"I consistently work on a mindset and attitude that keeps me moving forward."

The top 3 things I'm focusing on to help my brain protect my mindset and attitude are:

NEXT

Now, on to the final installment of your P.L.A.**N.**, but it's certainly not the end of your goal. In many ways, it's the signal to a new beginning since "N" is for *next.*

It's as simple and difficult as that. As in, focus on what's next. That's it. Just the next step. Why *just* the next step? Well, if you're anything like me, you'll otherwise get bogged down in details that only happen in your imagination, overwhelm yourself with "all" that you have to do, and then eventually come to the conclusion that usually leads to one of two outcomes: procrastination or giving up. Clearly, neither of those are places you want to land when formulating your exciting plan.

Conversely, when you focus only on *the next step* for your goal (big or small), then it's easier to actually achieve it. One achieved step builds some momentum, and that momentum sparks some confidence. Confidence is what keeps you going, progressing from one step to the next step, then the next, and the next, and ... That's it. Just rinse and repeat from there until you achieve your goal!

PRIORITIZED FOCUS

If I were to focus on *just the next* 1–3 steps for my goal, they would be:

Step #1

Step #2

Step #3

Not sure? Take a look at your *big* plan and work backward until you determine which step you are at in the process.

PUTTING YOUR P.L.A.N. TOGETHER

Now you've got a real P.L.A.N., isn't that exciting? Be sure that you use it! Use it to move forward and sharpen your Prioritized Focus skills!

Here's a brief recap before we move on to help you keep it clear and ready to execute. That's the most important part, right?

1. Get clear on the **P**urpose behind your goal.
2. Assign it a **L**ength of time.
3. Have the **A**ttitude needed to make progress.
4. Keep your focus on what's immediately **N**ext.

Just to be 1,000 percent sure that you are not at risk of over-complicating this, I want to paint an unlikely, but still practical, scenario for you.

Pretend it's Tuesday and I just called to inform you that I'm gifting you an all-expense-paid trip to some knock-your-socks-off destination for a week. The catch is you have to be ready to leave by Friday afternoon. How quickly do you think you could put a plan together to be ready by the deadline?

I'm pretty confident you would quickly prioritize what needed to be done—and do it—in order to enjoy a free trip. You have suddenly become a Prioritized Focus ninja with your time and tasks!

But in reality, we're more likely to overthink and overcomplicate things, aren't we? Well, you may want to grab a snack because I'm jumping right into another popular goal-getter mix-up that often trips us up.

VISION, MISSION AND GOALS

How clear are you on the differences between vision, mission, and goals? About as good as you were with passion + purpose, time management + methods, or mindset + attitude? Well, you're not alone if you admit they're a bit fuzzy. But you've hung with me this far, so you know we're about to make sure they're clear.

As you can probably guess, getting vision, mission, and goals mixed up or not having clarity about them can definitely mess with your goals, P.L.A.N., and your progress.

Yet, these three words—vision, mission, and goals—are used consistently to keep us on track and focused in our attempt to achieve our goals and ultimately our dream. This is great if you can distinguish the differences, but pretty frustrating if you can't.

Hang with me, I know this is a lot of information to not only take in, but also untangle. You're doing awesome! (And we're almost to those plug-and-play methods you've probably been itching to get to.)

YOUR VISION

To keep it as simple as possible, think of vision as the "far-off" dream that you have. And for all that we've covered so far, consider it the dream that you've been given and entrusted to achieve.

If I were to give you my best visual reference for vision (aka your dream), it would be a cloud. We know that clouds exist and can be seen, yet at the same time are not quite able to be grasped. That is very much like your vision. You may believe your God-given dream is "there," but you can't quite get hold of the whole picture.

In addition, clouds and our dreams can be seen as good and bad. What? Deana, are you saying we can think negatively about the vision for our life and future? Well, kinda ….

Clouds can be considered bad, especially when they severely impair visibility as fog or a rolling storm. One surefire way to cloud the vision for your life is to think it's never going to happen because of all of the obstacles (bad things) in the way. Those clouds appear too thick, too black, and carrying nothing but storms. Ever catch yourself thinking like that about your dream?

In contrast, a good way to view clouds is while lazily lying on the grass looking up. At that moment, your unhindered imagination sees nothing but fluffy, peaceful shapes floating by. A similar perspective could be applied to your vision/dream; the one you *want* to bring into the world because of the imagination, excitement, and even hope and peace it brings.

Do you see how that real but "untouchable" cloud is very much like your God-given dream? Just like the clouds, your dreams are a mix of rain and sun. They require both for growth, both physically and metaphorically. Thankfully, you get to choose the perspective you have about the hard stuff you endure, and enjoy the pleasant stuff when it comes to growing into who you are meant to be.

Dread and Dream contain just one letter difference, yet their meanings are a world apart.

YOUR MISSION

A mission is a special assignment given to you for the benefit of others. It's not about you.

A visual for mission is simply a heart. Your mission is the reason (heart) behind your dream. I love this part because whose heart is it that's behind *your* mission? God's! What's the special assignment He's given you to carry out? Yep, that God-given dream of yours.

God's mission for you comes by way of the dream He has given you. Your mission is to consistently grow into your God-given dream. When you do this, you're blessed, and more importantly, others truly benefit. The stronger you align with the heart behind your mission (His), the clearer your steps become as you walk out that mission.

Where there is a will, there is a way, right? Think of your mission as the day-to-day P.L.A.N. you execute to become the person specially assigned to carry it out.

DO NOTHING
OUT OF SELFISH
AMBITION OR VAIN
CONCEIT. RATHER,
IN HUMILITY VALUE
OTHERS ABOVE
YOURSELVES, NOT
LOOKING TO YOUR
OWN INTERESTS
BUT EACH OF YOU
TO THE INTERESTS
OF THE OTHERS.

- Philippians 2:3-4 NIV

Ever hear of a group of people being "on mission"? That's a fantastic way to describe a group of hearts collectively carrying out their assignments on purpose.

Take a few minutes to ponder and pray about your mission. We hear a lot about mission statements and their importance, probably because they really do help provide clarity and direction. Yet here's something I wish someone had told me: Your mission statement can change.

Think about it. If you are constantly growing and maturing into who you need to be in order to handle that God-given dream He's entrusted to you, wouldn't it make sense that your mission statement grows with you? I know mine has certainly changed over the years. My very first mission statement was an acronym (go figure!) and I still have it on a canvas in my office. It was GROW and stood for Give Reward Other Women, based on Philippians 2:3–4.

At the writing of this book, my current mission statement is: *Arming busy, overwhelmed women with the strategies to answer their God-sized callings with Prioritized Focus.* The core of my mission has remained, but with growth came more specificity. With that specificity, the day-to-day decisions are much easier to keep me focused and on mission!

If you don't feel ready for a mission statement just yet, focus on understanding what mission really means. And continue to connect the dots of all that we've covered so far. If you are getting a bit hung up on your "assigned who," don't worry; I've got you covered. We'll discuss that in the very next chapter. But for now, we're going to round out the last piece of the vision, mission, and goals trio.

YOUR GOALS

I know this is probably a tired analogy, but go with me anyway—think archery. The more an archer practices, the better she gets, right? She puts the arrow into the bow. She steadies her stance and breath, takes focus, aims, and releases the arrow in the direction of the target. And not just the target, but *the bullseye* in the center of the target.

Here's the part that is important and applies to us: The target is the direction of our aim. The bullseye is our point of focus and concentration. It's the goal. Our tasks are the arrows that represent our practice. The more intentional we get with our arrows, the more skilled we get at aiming our focus, and the closer we get to hitting our goal: the bullseye.

You may be thinking it all sounds simple enough, but what does that look like in real-life applications?

Well, here's my fresh take for you: This book is an example of just one of my goals. By "hitting that bullseye," it supports my mission (the heart behind what I do and why). That mission gets me closer to the ultimate vision that God intends for my faith, my life, and my business—through my dream.

So while it's more than fantastic to know and understand the role of vision, mission, and goals, it's paramount that you understand *your responsibility* in each of them and how they support one another.

PRIORITIZED FOCUS

Use this space to start thinking about:

YOUR VISION *(the cloud)*

YOUR MISSION *(the heart)*

YOUR GOAL(s) *(arrows, target, & bullseye)*

WHAT TO DO RIGHT NOW

Maybe you're experiencing information overload right now from this chapter or the entire book to this point. So I'm going to say something pretty unusual for an author to say to her readers: It's okay to take a pause.

Seriously, take the time to work through those feelings that follow choice. Are you choosing to overwhelm yourself to the point of giving up? Or are you choosing to recognize *what's right for you right now*? There's absolutely no guilt or judgment here. It's okay to take a pause.

Pray about it. Seriously, right here and now ask God to help you discover and then define what He's meant for you to understand *and* how to apply it *right now* to your life.

Maybe you're sure that now is the time to dig in and start implementing. And that may mean coming back and finishing the rest of the book later. It's okay to take a pause.

I get it. From information and concepts to definitions and discovering how many things you need to *un*learn, this chapter (and this book as a whole) can be *a lot*.

I'm here to remind and encourage you that this is a book, not a one-time seminar with schedule constraints, designated destinations, or outside distractions.

You can come back and go over paragraphs and chapters as often as you need. You can write notes and make highlights (If it's yours; that'd be awkward if you borrowed it. In that case, get a notebook).

→ I'm giving you permission to not treat this as some material you'll be tested on the moment you close the book. (← Pssst, you don't need my permission!)

By the way, I'm *so* proud of you and the work you have put into this process so far. This book may not have been the read you were expecting, but I hope that you are finding it worth your time and energy.

GROW U

That being said, I *am* going *to* push you to *apply and try what resonates.* Tweak, modify, and adapt what you need to in order to suit your situation. But VAL, please promise me that you *will* work to make progress toward *your goal!*

My prayer is that in sharing each "new" concept, experience, tactic, difference, encouragement, and resource, you are growing in knowledge. This knowledge can be used as the foundation to build your confidence as you go after that dream of yours; the one that God has entrusted to you.

There's one more discovery to address before we determine which day-to-day methods will move you closer to the kind of faith, life, and business you were meant to steward and share. It's time to piece together your right fit.

MY BUSINESS IS
NOT TO REMAKE
MYSELF BUT MAKE
THE ABSOLUTE
BEST OF WHAT
GOD MADE.

— *Robert Browning*

CHAPTER 8

Your Right Fit

PIECES, PEEPS, & PARTNERS

YOU ARE NOT EVERYBODY'S KIND OF SOMEBODY. If that last statement just stepped on a feeling, I'm sorry, but girl, you need to stop with the people pleasing! It's not only hurting you but also those you are meant to reach and help. Your MESSage is meant to be different. It's based on the unique experiences, perspectives, and ways you've been gifted to deliver it.

You need to get crystal clear on these for yourself or you'll be exhausting and frustrating yourself trying to be someone else's kind of somebody.

Resist the urge to defend yourself. Instead, lean into the MESSage and encouragement coming at you in this chapter.

I get it; I really do. We like to be liked. We want *everyone* to agree that our faith, products, accomplishments, or mission is great, beneficial, and needed. But even more than we want them to love *it*, we want them to love *us*.

To be liked *and* helpful? VAL, that's checking a lot of our D.O.S.E. boxes (see Chapter 4.5). But are those actually strengthening our desire and ability to be impactful or merely serving as short-term fixes?

The goal of this chapter is to go beyond people pleasing and nailing your niche, tracking your tribe, creating your perfect avatar, or finally finding your target market. These are what the industry gurus are sending you on a wild chase to find. This chapter, my friend, is about helping you align your God-given dream with those who've been assigned to be a part of it.

MESSAGES

Alignment between who you're becoming and the dream God's entrusted you with is less about finding the right people and more about serving those God has assigned you to share your MESSage.

I say MESSage because that's usually how we see ourselves, our lives, our work/business: a big ol' mess. But really, our self-proclaimed messy lives are God's favorite way to prove to us that's just not the case.

He separates the perfection we pursue and how we want to be perceived from what really resonates with and has the most impact on others: our messy circumstances and experiences. Then He turns them into an impactful, helpful, and fulfilling MESSage, as only He can. I mean, what's more relatable to another person than the tie of life's messiness?

PUZZLED

In this chapter, we will be honing in on discovering who you've been assigned to serve, what MESSage you've been prepped and equipped to deliver, and why it matters for you and your assignees.

It's fun for me to watch how creative VALs can get once that MESSage piece of the puzzle has been put into place. Speaking of puzzles, I just thought of an analogy. Let's run with it and see where it goes! (Rolls her eyes with a grimace and goes for it anyway.)

Think of your dream as the picture on the front of the puzzle box; that's the dream (vision) God has given you. Remember, your vision/dream is that far-off thing that's like a cloud; you can see it, but not quite reach or touch it. At the same time, you know that it's real and meant for *you*.

As it turns out, that beautiful picture on the front of the puzzle box *is exactly what you would have imagined* had you thought of it! That's the way it is with God; He always has better in store for us than what we could come up with on our own. He crafts ways to remind us and point us to that "picture on the box." His picture for you, customized piece by piece in a specially designed "box" (plan) just for you. It's exactly what He created for you to complete.

But ... some of us never get past looking at the picture once we receive the box. Instead, we spend more time daydreaming about the dream/vision we were given than actively and intentionally putting the pieces together. We're excited and inspired, but that's where it ends.

Why? Is it because we look at the total number of pieces and suddenly realize the amount of work it will actually take to put that amazing picture together? *Ugh!* And just like that, we allow what we see—the messy pieces—to doubt what God revealed to us and says He has for us.

Instead of focusing on the beautiful, potential outcome before us, we choose to see a whole list of *what-ifs* that prevents us from even pulling the lid off that box, let alone pursuing it to completion.

Just like that, we go from excitement to overwhelm.

PIECE BY PIECE

Continuing with our puzzle analogy (it's going well so far, so why not continue, right?), think of the steps you typically take when it comes to putting together the picture on the box.

First, you start flipping the pieces over so you can identify clues as to where they might fit into the big picture. Then you sort or group them in a way that makes sense to you. The hope is that it will make it easier to recognize where pieces may go later.

Next, maybe you start to pull out all of the "edge pieces" so that you can begin constructing the outer border. You do this knowing that once this part is done, the rest of the pieces fit somewhere inside that framework, which will ultimately hold the entire puzzle together. (Have you ever given thought to what's holding your entire dream/vision together?)

Finally, you do your best to find where the rest of the pieces fit together within the outer border/framework. It's trial and error at this point. The cool part about this step is that the order doesn't really matter! The goal is to complete the puzzle. Will it take you a day, a week, months, or even years? That depends on you and how much time and effort you commit to working on your puzzle.

What do you do when a piece looks like it "goes there" but doesn't quite fit? Throw the whole puzzle away? Of course not. You put it aside to try again later and go work on another area. The same is true for piecing together your big-picture vision. You'll learn from what doesn't work properly, and come back and try again later after other pieces have been properly placed. It doesn't mean that the piece is wrong, but maybe the timing isn't ready yet for that particular piece to fall into place.

There's no real easy way to speed up this part of the process. It's literally moving and working piece by piece. However, the more you practice, the more comfortable you'll be with the process. You also become faster with the process and dare I say, the whole process becomes easier. Oh, and get this: You'll be better equipped and experienced to handle bigger puzzles next time. Huh, just like life—imagine that!

Pursuing the dream/vision may be our goal, but do you want to know what God's goal is in all of this? *Seeing us become who He created us to be through the process; His process.*

How many times have you walked away in frustration, both from a literal puzzle and the dream that God has given you? Guess what? Most of that frustration comes from a lack of progress. Actually, if we're really truthful, it's because the progress just isn't fast enough for us. And the worst reason, which may be a bit embarrassing once you figure it out, is when you try to put your pieces into someone else's puzzle.

In those *moments* of lack of progress, we have to ask ourselves: "Is it because I've neglected to take the time to stop and look at the 'big picture'—the one that He gave me and entrusted me with?"

BUT I'M TIRED. . .

There's something else about vision that I waited to share with you until now because it ties into understanding this big picture.

In our desire for speedy gratification, we neglect to realize something important. Are you ready for this one?

Here it is: When you think of what success looks like in light of your dream/vision, think in terms of the fact that *it should outlive you.*

Whoa! Hold. the. phone.

Don't throw the book across the room or give up reading the rest of it ... stick with me here. It's not that you won't live your dream or see your vision come to fruition in your lifetime, it's just *bigger* than your life. In other words, if you're pursuing your God-given dream the way He created you to, it should outlive you.

What do you think about that? I hope it inspires you to think a bit differently, more intentionally.

VAL, when you start thinking of your dream/vision in terms of legacy building, the day-to-day decision process becomes easier. Motivation isn't hiding like your dog trying to get out of a bath. And the fear of what others think of your pursuit of your vision/dream – well, that becomes their problem, not yours.

IF YOU'RE PURSUING YOUR GOD-GIVEN DREAM THE WAY HE CREATED YOU TO, IT SHOULD OUTLIVE YOU.

YOUR PEEPS

When it comes to our puzzles (I can't believe I'm going this far with the whole puzzle/dream analogy, but we're too deep to stop now!), both the physical, put-together-kind and the one as it relates to our vision/dream, we have to remember that *others can contribute*.

Others can contribute by putting pieces into place to help you complete your puzzle—*even though it's not theirs*. They're happy to find a piece that fits and put it in its place; they find satisfaction and a sense of fulfillment by helping you.

But they can only do this when you share the big picture with them. Remember what we said about mission in the last chapter? Mission is the heart behind all that you're doing in order to make progress toward your God-given dream, but it's also very much about the hearts it reaches in the process.

Sure, sometimes we get mad because we wanted to take all the credit for doing it by ourselves. Or maybe we get mad *because* they left us to do it on our own. When this happens, it's because we've lost sight of the ultimate goal: finishing. That *is* the ultimate goal, right?

You see, once we share the big picture/vision/dream with others, things start to shift. We'll find that some of our peeps help us make progress while others hurt or hinder us in our pursuit. Whether it's by their actions or words, we have to be prepared to handle both those who help and those who hurt or hinder. We have to remember the big picture when someone comes along and says something to us like:

- That's already been done, so why are you even bothering?
- If it's so hard for/on you, why not save yourself the time and trouble and stop?

- I think that it's too late, too big, too small ... for you to be doing this.
- Clearly, you're too old (or young or inexperienced, etc.).

Are any of those striking a chord with you right now? They do with me. I've heard them, too, in my mind and with my ears.

Instead of getting frustrated or offended, consider that maybe they just aren't the audience to whom God has assigned you to share your MESSage. Taking it a step further, which will maybe give you some peace of mind, know that God has every one of the somebodies that you are assigned to reach ready to hear your MESSage.

God already has every one of the somebodies that you are assigned to reach ready to hear your MESSage.

But, if you keep delaying the discovery and sharing of *your* MESSage, they will be delayed in stepping into and discovering *their* assigned MESSage. You know, that "beautiful picture on the front of the box" customized just for you. And here's an important fact to remember: You can do this while still piecing that picture together. VAL (Valued, Amazing Lady), read that again because that was for you to understand. Realize it's an ongoing process; this is not a one-and-done event. It's growth that happens piece by piece. Some of those pieces are people, some are events and circumstances, and others have to do with sitting still in His presence and listening for further instructions.

PERMISSION

You don't need permission to pursue your God-given, for-you, dream. But I will give you a *friendly push* to focus less on your "ideal somebody" and more on your MESSage and those you've been assigned to share it with.

Once you are able to wrap your heart and mind around your assigned MESSage, the next step is to discover the medium in which to share it. The potential impact your MESSage can have is incredibly more than you could even imagine *if* you learn to use the time and medium God has planned for you.

Think about what that might look like for you. As I type these words onto a virtual document and watch the cursor blink and move, it's not lost on me that my medium is sharing encouragement through words, whether I'm writing them or speaking them.

How would you ever come to read these words, this MESSage, if I never made the time to write them to you? Oh, I absolutely believe they are to you, VAL.

Before I ever started this project, I prayed for you. I prayed that you would find just what you needed within these pages, right now where you are.

I may never get the privilege of meeting you, but I know that I'm the MESSenger that was assigned to you. In the middle of my own messy life journey, writing from my messy desk, I was assigned to encourage you, inspire you, and even help restore your faith that may be in need of serious repair right now. The God-given dream that's been entrusted to me and that has the potential to long outlive me is to share how and why to focus on your MESSage.

Does this mean I'm confident that I'm doing it right? Nope. Does it mean that I don't have fears and doubts that creep up? Nope, I do. People will criticize me and the work I know I've been assigned to do, but here's the thing: I trust the Designer of dreams, the Creator of my assigned craft, and the Authority over what I'm inspired to write. I know that you've been assigned to me at this moment, and me to you. The same is true for you and your assignment! My job right now is to encourage and arm you with the confidence and tools you need to stop delaying your pursuit!

So if you were looking for a permission slip, here it is, along with prayers, high-fives, "go-get-'em-girl" cheers, and a big ol' smile with tears of joy. All for *you*!

Your assignment is waiting on you. They're ready to receive the MESSage you've been assigned to share with them in the way you've been best designed to do it.

PARTNERSHIPS

In terms of our culture, partnerships are the best way to get your MESSage heard at the right time and place to the right people. It's also the fastest way for peeps to find you. Not just any people, but *your* right peeps; those that have been assigned to you. If you're ever going to put that puzzle together, you'll need the right kinds of partnerships. Ones that can help those peeps easily find their way to you.

Before we get into those criteria, there is one partnership that needs to be prioritized first and foremost in all that you do. Without this one, you'll just be rearranging the pieces without ever really finding where they fit.

This partnership isn't about going 50/50, either; it's got to be *all in*, 100 percent of you.

Ever heard the phrase, *"God's got this"*? Well, that's the most factual part of your partnership with Him. When you truly believe that He's got *your* whole puzzle figured out, *you'll be way more patient in the process.* Your Partner's just waiting on you to follow His guidance.

Even when you lose sight of the big picture, all the pieces are still there. It may take longer to flip, try, and arrange the pieces, but if you're patient, put in the work, and trust your Partner, you *will* see results.

That may sound all fine and good, but when you need tangible help, support, resources, and tools, what do you do?

First, ask Him to help you recognize what's needed and show you the way to what's He's already provided *for* you! Novel concept, huh? Listen, I don't know of anyone who can overcomplicate or overthink a situation more than *moi*, so trust me when I tell you this absolutely works!

There is a bit of a caveat, though: It most likely won't happen on your timeline. Or even in the way you might expect. But if it's part of your puzzle He has for you, you'll get it!

Before I ever knew I was going to make writing a key component of my business, my Partner knew. Years ago, He put a brilliant writer and now a writing coach, Dalene, in the same business mastermind as me. She was just as frustrated and fearful of entrepreneurship as I was, yet we both knew God called us to it. Now we are great friends, and there isn't a writing project I do without seeking her support, critique, and guidance. That was a piece of my big picture I didn't even know about at the time, all those years ago. But my Partner did.

The same has been true in my spiritual growth, health and fitness goals, and other areas of my life and business, where relationships seemed random and not even close to being connected to my big picture at the time. But now, looking back, it's easy to see how and why my Partner orchestrated those pieces to fit.

Some of these partnerships happened organically, while others I have sought out and paid to be mentored, coached, taught, or tutored by them. I want to point this out because we can often be told and led to believe that as Christians, we can sit back and God will handle all the work. I could fill up pages with arguments to the contrary. I mean, David still had to fight Goliath, the Israelites had to fight for their Promised Land, the disciples still had to follow and learn from Jesus, and Jesus went to and endured the cross *for* us ... The key here is to know your part and, more importantly, who you are meant to partner with.

The more you trust your Partner, the more clarity you get on your dream/vision, those you're meant to serve, the MESSage you are meant to share, and how to share it. It also becomes easier to determine where the partners that have been sent your way fit!

VAL, stop leaving your dream/vision to chance. It's time to step into who you were created to be. Open the lid on your big-picture puzzle box and start flipping the pieces.. You're equipped enough to share the MESSage you were assigned and your peeps are waiting. Trust your Partner and the partnerships He provides. Now it's time to look at your positioning and take control of your part.

Part 3

DETERMINE

GETTING PRACTICAL & TACTICAL IN YOUR FAITH, LIFE & BUSINESS

HEY, YOU VALUED, Amazing Lady, you – you're doing great! You've completed the first two parts of this book.

We are now turning a corner, VAL. While the majority of the book is about mindset and perspective shifts, that first half was really about helping you dig into and do that hard, but necessary inner work. This next section is about giving you practical and repeatable ways to uphold that right mindset and make progress in *your* right direction. (not just any)

SEE, I AM DOING A NEW THING! NOW IT SPRINGS UP; DO YOU NOT PERCEIVE IT? I AM MAKING A WAY IN THE DESERT AND STREAMS IN THE WASTELAND.

- Isaiah 43:19 NIV

CHAPTER 9

Taking Control

OLD FAITH'S NOT
ENOUGH FOR NEW PROBLEMS

Do **YOU FEEL THE NEED TO CONTROL JUST ABOUT EVERYTHING?** I used to be very much of a control freak! Okay, so I still have some control freak tendencies and "episodes" from time to time, but they're definitely less frequent since I learned what trying to control everything really meant. This knowledge changed my perspective and helped me loosen my grip on control. (Hey, loosened is better than a death grip—remember, I still have tendencies. Progress, VAL, progress.) I believe this knowledge can help you relax your grip on control a bit more, too.

Wanting to control everything is rooted in ... *fear*. Fear of what? Well, friend, that answer is as individual as we are, but might include fears like:

- not feeling safe,
- not being the leader or person in charge,
- not being the source of making others "happy" (Uh-oh. D.O.S.E. dip?),
- not having the freedom to do what you want.

Controlling your priorities, time, and emotions is a good thing. Please don't think I'm talking about letting that all go by the wayside by any means.

As a matter of fact, this chapter is all about making decisions based on your priorities from a place of intention and purpose rather than out of fears and feelings. When you can handle those, you'll be able to not only find, but keep your focus!

So let me ask you: Do you *really* need to be in control or is there a fear you're hiding behind? Take some time and think of the things you Just. Have. To. Control. Then get honest about why.

THE POWER OF ONE

What's your *one*? The one "thing" that changed other things. Perhaps it was one choice, one year, one word, one smile, or maybe it was just taking one more step when you didn't think you had it in you that changed a situation, perspective, time, place, or even a person. Did you ever stop to think about the power of *just one* for yourself?

For me, there have been a lot of "ones" that have altered my direction, perspective, and influence; some I've already shared with you. They've led to both good and not-so-good outcomes, depending on which "one."

But, in some way, I've come to realize that those "ones" have gotten me to where I am today. And for that, I am thankful. Thankful because I've realized there's power in those "ones;" regardless of whether I thought that they were big or small, they've all been impactful.

I've also realized that those "ones" were also catalysts. For example, one decision was to begin blogging. That "one" led to so many other things: Writing this book, coaching others, speaking, and even training with bigger organizations!

One of the first blogs I ever published was called Redemption Season. I go back to it often not just to see how far I've come as a writer, but because I need the reminder that it's true, especially since it seems I require some sort of redemption *every* day, not just in a season! How about you?

Hey, it's never about how many times we get knocked down; it's how many times we get *up*, right?! Sometimes those falls can be embarrassing and even messy, but I promise it's better to get up rather than just lying there waiting to be picked up! (That's more embarrassing; trust me on that one.)

Lately, I've been feeling a bit emotional—not in a boo-hoo kind of way, but in a restorative, reflective kind of way. You see, by stepping into my assignment as a writer, I've embraced and now value the way God designed me. Yes, beyond the titles, labels, and history that we talked about way back in Chapter 3.

By accepting His assignment for me, I'm finding more and more women have forgotten who they are and were created to be. VAL, you and I have got to do a better job of pulling ourselves together. (Is anyone else picturing Edna Mode from the movie *The Incredibles*, right now?)

We need to remember that *we are* Valued Amazing Ladies, created on purpose, for a purpose.

So VAL, if you are feeling knocked down, uninspired, or even unsupported, please know that I'm praying for you and I'm pulling for you. You are the reason I write, speak, coach, and train—all in an effort to encourage you (and those like you) in faith, everyday life, and business.

PRESSING IN & ON

Maybe you're thinking, "What's this life I'm living all for? How do I know if I'm on the right track?" Those are valid questions and concerns, ones that I hope you find clarity about through Christ as we continue our journey together in this book … as well as later on your own.

Remember in Chapter 7 when we took an in-depth discovery of your vision, mission, and goals? Well, I thought this would be a good spot to share mine with you. Not for it to serve as a distraction or become a fill-in-the-blank version for you to copy and compare, but for you to see that I'm still on my journey and navigating this process, too. Even as I write this, I feel that my vision, mission, and goals are a constant work in progress. By sharing them and their state as of now, I hope they will encourage you as you consider yours. Know that it's okay to revisit them, pray for clarity, and make adjustments as God gives you that clarity!

I PRESS ON TO
REACH THE END
OF THE RACE
AND RECEIVE THE
HEAVENLY PRIZE
FOR WHICH GOD,
THROUGH CHRIST
JESUS, IS CALLING
US.

- Philippians 3:14 NLT

MY VISION: This is the someday goal that was literally a vision given to me by the Holy Spirit during a time of prayer more than a decade ago. Thanks to my renewed willingness to seek growth over stuck-ness, I'm getting better at articulating it!

> *To ignite a movement that creates a desire to go beyond just a study of God's Word. One that people will have the desire to discover and pursue knowing who God really is, on a personalized level to the point that they just can't shut up about or show up to work without Him. They are recognizing and sharing their MESSage because of the one He's entrusted to me.*

MY MISSION: This is the everyday goal that no matter what's happening, I can do something to move the mission forward. It's displaying the heart behind what I'm doing in order to touch others' hearts.

Personal Mission to remind me of my entrusted MESSAGE:

> *To create meaningful, thought-provoking content. Words that compel, inspire, and restore faith and focus to the spiritually weary and moody Christian women (like me, both in attitude & hormones).*

This version is to remind me what I'm to do, why, and to whom.

Public Mission to share who my assigned MESSage is for:

Arming overwhelmed and busy women in business with strategies to answer their God-sized calling with prioritized focus.

MY GOALS: These are the meaningful and tangible milestones I can use to uphold the vision and propel the mission.

Use this book, You're A Beautiful Messterpiece, as a tool, resource, and catalyst for encouraging others. Continue to write, speak, and create resources that further the vision and mission on the front of my "puzzle box."

Now it's your turn, VAL. What can you do—or continue to do—to step into your assignment as the Valued Amazing Lady you are? It's okay to take a moment to reflect on all that you're feeling right now. As a matter of fact, I encourage you to record it somewhere in a notebook, a voice memo, a journal, your planner ....

Here's some space in case you can't trust yourself to stay focused on the way to finding a piece of paper!

QUICK THOUGHTS TO NOTE:

That should be enough to hold you over until you're really ready to map it all out. You're doing great and I'm so proud of all the work that you've put in so far. You're really gaining some momentum!

SEEING, TRUTHING & TRANSITIONING

Since the 2020 COVID pandemic of epic proportions, there have been plenty of things to be grumpy and gripe about, especially if you follow *any* type of media. Yet it's also offered the opportunity to reevaluate your perspectives and use them to change your future. How'd ya do?

Whether it's the pandemic, politics, or anything else, you have the power to choose if seeing is believing or believing is seeing.

If another season of quarantine or some other global issue were to appear on the horizon, how would you see it?

- *See* it as being stuck at home or blessed to be home and not in a hospital bed?
- *See* truck drivers, delivery people, cashiers, janitors, teachers, officers, and first responders as vital to everyday life, or continue to see other jobs as "more important"?
- *See* freedoms as a right or privilege that comes with both a cost and sacrifice?

Remember back in Chapter 4 when we looked at change and making decisions? When you want something to change, you have to make a decision. Too often, though, we want (and wait for) someone to come along and give us a direction to go when really, it's about making a decision based on what we already know. Decisions provide direction.

> *No matter how global the issue or the one affecting our own smaller worlds, we have the power to prioritize our focus.*

Seeing what good can come based on the everyday choices that we make would be a good priority to have. Not sure which choices to start with? How about just being kind to one another? All the way back in Chapter 1 we talked about the importance of bearing fruit. Kindness is one of the nine universal "fruits" that everyone has the ability to bear and share.

We act what we believe, so VAL, you'd better learn to become a truth finder, especially when it comes to your beliefs! This means being sure you understand what you believe about yourself versus what God's truth says about you. Do they align? Only then will you know if you're speaking the truth *to and about yourself.* Which, by the way, may be the hardest of all levels to master.

For me, all truth is God's truth and He always manages to prove those truths to me. He is the original Master and Teacher. The following passage is about what it takes to armor up and handle what we see and believe.

Not sure where you are in your journey? That's okay, just know that you're right on time! The best thing to do is lean into that feeling and then, *ask, seek, and knock.*

THEREFORE PUT ON THE FULL ARMOR
OF GOD, SO THAT WHEN THE DAY OF
EVIL COMES, YOU MAY
BE ABLE TO STAND YOUR GROUND,
AND AFTER YOU HAVE
DONE EVERYTHING, TO STAND.

STAND FIRM THEN, WITH THE BELT
OF TRUTH BUCKLED AROUND YOUR
WAIST, WITH THE BREASTPLATE OF
RIGHTEOUSNESS IN PLACE, AND WITH
YOUR FEET FITTED

WITH THE READINESS THAT COMES
FROM THE GOSPEL OF PEACE. IN
ADDITION TO ALL THIS, TAKE UP
THE SHIELD OF FAITH, WITH WHICH
YOU CAN EXTINGUISH ALL THE
FLAMING ARROWS OF THE EVIL ONE.
TAKE THE HELMET OF SALVATION
AND THE SWORD OF THE SPIRIT,
WHICH IS THE WORD OF GOD.

- Ephesians 6:13-17 NIV

(EMPHASIS ADDED)

Most of us have been both inspired and disappointed by this ask, seek, knock verse at some point in our lives. Probably because we've heard it as

- encouragement to go after what you want,
- a reason why you are not getting what you want,
- a mantra to grow your business, ministry, or reach,
- a way for God to answer your prayer.

> ## "ASK AND IT WILL BE GIVEN TO YOU; SEEK AND YOU WILL FIND; KNOCK AND THE DOOR WILL BE OPENED TO YOU."
>
> *— Matthew 7:7-8 NIV*
> **(EMPHASIS ADDED)**

These three words—ask, seek, and knock—have often been prescribed as the go-to of how-tos in getting an answer or giving a direction. Ask, seek, knock ... been there, done that. Now what?

Part of my morning routine is to spend time quietly reading, writing, and reflecting. This has proven to be one of my most powerful practices. It keeps me focused on making progress in my assignment. During one of my morning readings, this "old familiar" Bible verse of ask, seek, knock hit me with a very new mindset shift.

Before I get to the part that stood out and changed my perspective (and maybe yours, too), let me first go back and share the two things that I already knew to be true about this passage (and maybe you do, too):

1. Ask, seek, and knock are all *actions*; things that you can choose to do (or not do). Your actions are the things that are within your control.

2. Given, find, and open are the corresponding *outcomes*. While you can do your best to predict outcomes, you cannot control them.

In a nutshell, your actions are within your control but their outcomes are not.

Here's the one little word that stood out to me that particular morning; a word that is repeated after each expected action and just before the promised result: *will*.

The word "will" has two meanings, which represent the *secret* and the *catch*:

- expressing future tense
- expressing inevitable events

This means that sometimes you have to take the additional and uncomfortable *action* of waiting before receiving, finding, and opening the door!

Although many of us act as if we are unable to move unless we get the answer we want, need, or hope for, the reality is that *we can actively wait.*

Even now, knowing this insight, most of us look at the actions of asking, seeking, and knocking as having "put in the work." By the time we say, "amen," we're ready for the results. Or so we think ....

Will the results happen tomorrow? Maybe.

Next week? Possibly.

In a month? Perhaps.

One, two, or five years from now?!

"Tell me already?!" is what the mind often wants to scream. But the truth is ... the placement of that little word, "will," means it's out of your control. Your asking, seeking, and knocking *will* pay off; you just don't know when. God's the only One who knows and His timing is impeccable, whether you agree in the moment or not. You just have to remember to hold onto the promise that it *will* happen.

Something else very important to note here, which may be a bit of a caveat for some, is that asking, seeking, and knocking need to be in alignment with God's character (see Psalm 145—whew!), His will, and His Word. So be sure that you are intimately familiar with those so you can be patiently expectant rather than frustrated and disappointed.

The beauty of it is that if you're intimately familiar with Him, you won't ask for anything that's outside of His character, will, or Word. For some, that may seem too tall an order, but for others, it's just the spark needed to start praying some *bold*er prayers!

Let's not be ones to abandon asking, seeking, or knocking because nothing has happened *yet.* Is there even a time frame on

WHEN YOU
PRIORITIZE YOUR
FOCUS ON WHO
YOU NEED TO
BECOME IN ORDER
TO HANDLE WHAT
IT IS YOU'RE
ASKING, SEEKING,
AND KNOCKING, IT
MAKES YOU READY
FOR THE OUTCOME
GOD HAS PREPARED
FOR YOU.

"yet"? Remember, God gets to determine the time frame of what *will* happen … and when.

That stinking little word, "will," changed my whole outlook on how I pray. I was finally able to recognize that a *transition* needs to happen before a *transaction* of any desired outcome can take place.

WHINING OR WINNING

After grasping the whole ask, seek, knock mindset shift, you'd think it would be smooth sailing, right? Well, if you're anything like me and other weary and often moody Christians out there, you'll soon find yourself whining to God about things like:

- God, am I even on the right track?
- God, did I hear You correctly in this?
- God, what if I can't do it?
- God, why is this so hard?

I know I'm not the only one who has had these types of "conversations" with God—even after a brand-new mindset shift! But God is so patient and loving. He just keeps pointing us in the direction He wants us to go. His directions can be through our circumstances, a song or message, and especially through His Word.

For example, when I found myself quickly questioning God (okay, whining to Him) after my ask, seek, knock epiphany, I was divinely led to the following verses:

"BLESSED IS SHE WHO HAS BELIEVED THAT WHAT THE LORD HAS SAID TO HER WILL BE ACCOMPLISHED!"

— *Luke 1:45 NIV*

(EMPHASIS ADDED)

"MAY THE LORD DIRECT YOUR HEARTS INTO GOD'S LOVE AND CHRIST'S PERSEVERANCE."

– 2 Thessalonians 3:5 NIV
(EMPHASIS ADDED)

Well, that was humbling. That moment was another truth confirmation: He speaks. He sees. He encourages us to trust that He's got "this" (whatever your current "this" is). He knows what control freaks we can be, how good we are at the "what-if" scenarios, and how quick we are at pointing out exactly who and what is against us (that finger rarely points toward us, does it?).

It's best if you can focus on

- staying in *your* lane,
- paying attention to *your* assignment, and
- doing *your* best.

When you do that based on what you have and know *right now,* I promise God will meet you where you are with the truth that you need.

IN WITH THE NEW

The subtitle of this chapter is: *Old Faith's Not Enough for New Problems.* If that's too vague or passive for you, the goal was to gently nudge you out of your comfort zone. After all, "old faith" is a type of code for a comfort zone, is it not? And you and I have lived long enough to know that there's always a new problem needing our particular attention every day.

I'm about to share something that may be a new concept to you: There's no such thing as an old problem, just a bad habit you've learned to tolerate. Let me say it again for the people in the back:

An old problem is a bad habit that you've learned to tolerate.

Therefore, "old problems" need to be replaced with good habits. New problems need solutions, which only come from action. And actions come from beliefs. Do you see where this is going?

We looked earlier at the power of one. Whether that's one choice, one day, or one step, that one little (or big) thing can make a difference. Then we talked about choosing to see. Well, that is a decision in itself. Will you see to believe or believe in order to see?

And finally, we considered truth—the importance of learning and finding it for yourself *(and armoring up at it!).*

VAL, no one can tell you what your dream is or what your success looks like. One has been assigned to you and the other is defined by your focus and your goals. But no matter how out of control things may seem or even be around us, we get to choose where to prioritize our focus. And truth be told, focus is the only way to achieve any goal!

In the next section of this book, that's exactly what we are going to learn how to implement—F.O.C.U.S. It's the only way to win your way to your goals every day in your faith, in your life, and in your business. Let's determine to do just that!

CHAPTER 10

Faith F.O.C.U.S.

THE FIRST AND MOST FOUNDATIONAL PART OF FINDING YOUR FOCUS

ACHIEVING ANY GOAL COMES FROM CONSIS-
TENTLY IMPROVING FOCUS. This area of improvement has
been at the forefront of my own faith, life, and business goal-getting for the last several years. It has also been foundational in my
content, coaching, and courses. The stronger my faith, the bolder
and more confident I become in those 3 C's—content, coaching,
and courses. It's an interesting pattern.

In this chapter and the two following, you'll get the secret sauce
behind the F.O.C.U.S. method—what it is and how it can help

IT IS LIKE A PERSON
BUILDING A HOUSE
WHO DIGS DEEP
AND LAYS THE
FOUNDATION ON
SOLID ROCK. WHEN
THE FLOODWATERS
RISE AND BREAK
AGAINST THAT
HOUSE, IT STANDS
FIRM BECAUSE IT IS
WELL BUILT.

– Luke 6:48 NLT

improve your own focus in your faith, life, and even your ministry, organization, or business.

All of the previous chapters have set you up for success in this F.O.C.U.S. area. So if you put in the work there, you're ready for what's next. I'm excited for you!

Only recently did I discover a "sticky" way to articulate this foundational practice of consistently improving focus. And by "sticky," I mean conveying the concepts in a simplified way so that they are remembered by the people who hear them.

The discovery came while I was creating content for a new group coaching program I called Fearless Focus. It was really an experiment, as most of my ventures are until they're tweaked a few times and proven by repeatable results. The ultimate goal was to provide a step-by-step process to help my assigned VALs overcome the usual suspects and obstacles that keep them distracted from their goals. It was a primitive version of the previous chapters of this book, and the foundation for what you're about to read next.

UNDERSTANDING THE F.O.C.U.S. METHOD

As one who loves a good acronym, I can't believe this simple concept of creating one from what I was teaching (i.e., focus) didn't come to me sooner than it did! Nevertheless, it finally did and you're about to see what I mean.

The F.O.C.U.S. methods for faith and life will likely be something completely new for you; it was a surprise to *me* how they came together ... and I created them! (I can't put my focus into practice without them now.) But the F.O.C.U.S. method for business may seem a little more familiar because it's more of an adaptation of common and proven methods.

Well, here we go! We're going to walk through this acronym together, letter by letter, until you have a full understanding of the F.O.C.U.S. method.

YOUR FAITH F.O.C.U.S.

I believe that your faith is the most important element of your focus; after all, it's belief *in* action! So the best way to keep your actions on track is to keep your faith in F.O.C.U.S.

For me, this was the missing link to all of my unmet expectations, unfinished projects, and underachieved goals. It has now become the foundation that enables me to get out of any rut, cycle of defeat, or procrastination season that I find myself in. I pray it helps you, too.

FAITH *F*.O.C.U.S.
F is for Fix it.

When something is broken, we are faced with the choice to either try and fix it, throw it away, or give it to someone else who wants it in its current state. Our faith is not much different.

If you feel that your faith is broken, you have those same options. It's up to you to make a choice. You can opt to try to fix it yourself, throw it away, or give it to God to meet you where you are in your current state.

Make no mistake, He is the one who will always want us in our current state, no matter how broken or how messed up we think we are. Do you find it comforting and amazing that God gives us those options? I do! But it gets better! He also gives us the promise of *how* it can be fixed.

When the decision is made to try and fix something that's broken or messed up, we have to determine where to start. When it comes to broken faith, the best starting point is not a place, but a Person.

THEREFORE, HOLY BROTHERS AND SISTERS, WHO SHARE IN THE HEAVENLY CALLING, FIX YOUR THOUGHTS ON JESUS, WHOM WE ACKNOWLEDGE AS OUR APOSTLE AND HIGH PRIEST.

— *Hebrews 3:1 NIV*
(EMPHASIS ADDED)

There's so much that we could unpack in this verse. However, for the sake of staying on topic, we're going to look at "fix your thoughts on Jesus."

First, your thoughts. If you've read this far, you recognize that thoughts are very much attached to your beliefs. What you believe, you act upon. So if you aren't sure of your beliefs, take a good look at your actions and vice versa.

Why should you fix your thoughts on Jesus? The very next phrase in this verse answers this question: "… whom we acknowledge as our apostle and high priest."

An apostle means one who is sent. A high priest connects his assigned people to God. Therefore, *if* you acknowledge Jesus as the One who was sent for the purpose of providing a way for you to be restored and never separated from God, *then* that also makes Jesus our advocate.

Oh, and how cool is it that *we* are Jesus's assignment?! We've talked about our assigned people; the best part is that He is our example of how to effectively connect with them! And get this:

He is the MESSiah (anointed one) and His story, the one we get to tell, is the Gospel MESSage of love, redemption, and hope!

Do you need a minute to let that sink in? Are you now understanding and appreciating the particular order of this book, about the process and inner work that is needed before we can ever hope to get to the outer part of living our dream through our lives and businesses?

BUT WAIT! THERE'S MORE...FOR US.

In the same book of Hebrews, we find yet another reason our thoughts should be fixed on Jesus: He's the founder and perfecter of our faith. Jesus's life and death on our behalf is literally the foundation of what we as Christians believe, and He perfected how to live that life.

The next verses point out that He endured shame, hostility, and the cross (the most brutal and humiliating way to die) *for us*.

His joy was knowing that it was *for us*. But He didn't just die for us—He defeated death forever. His death and resurrection gave us the option to also have victory over death. I don't know what you've got going on in your life, or how defeated you are feeling right now, but VAL, can you think of anything more powerful than defeating death? I can't. And the One who did that is *for* you, *for* me, *for* us.

He did it to pave the way for us so we wouldn't give up, but instead, focus on what was ahead of us. This requires us to put our belief and trust *in* Him, not just *about* Him. If we can do that, then when "death" comes for us, it's just a change in geography. We'll end up sitting with Him right next to God in heaven.

I hope this puts so much more purpose and passion behind that God-given dream of yours, especially when you come to the realization that your assignment includes pointing as many people as you can to Him, too, while you're still here on earth. Remember, we *are* His Kingdom here on earth. Eternity with Him began the moment our eyes fixed on Jesus and we said *yes* to Him as Lord and Savior.

LOOKING TO JESUS, THE
FOUNDER AND PERFECTER
OF OUR FAITH, WHO FOR
THE JOY THAT WAS SET
BEFORE HIM ENDURED
THE CROSS, DESPISING
THE SHAME, AND IS
SEATED AT THE RIGHT
HAND OF THE THRONE OF
GOD. CONSIDER HIM WHO
ENDURED FROM SINNERS
SUCH HOSTILITY AGAINST
HIMSELF, SO THAT YOU
MAY NOT GROW WEARY
OR FAINTHEARTED.

- Hebrews 12: 2-3 ESV
(EMPHASIS ADDED)

PUTTING THE FIX INTO PRACTICE

Once you commit to fixing your faith and understand Who should be the focus, you can then learn how to apply it to your day-to-day life.

> *Let your eyes look straight ahead;*
> *fix your gaze directly before you.*
>
> **- PROVERBS 4:25 NIV**
> *(emphasis added)*

I love the straightforwardness of this verse. First, it offers an option (*let* your eyes look straight ahead) and then a command (*fix* your gaze directly before you).

When my oldest daughter began taking horseback riding lessons, one of the first things she was taught was to look where she wanted the horse to go. She quickly learned that even if she was "pointing the horse straight" by keeping her reins steady, the direction would change if she turned her head. My son learned this lesson when learning to ride his dirt bike, too. The same is true for us, VAL.

If you find yourself not going in the direction that you want or should be going, take a serious look at your thoughts (the eyes of your mind) because those are what are directing your actions. Those actions are a reflection of what you're looking at. It's a simple solution, yet it's one that most often trips us up and steers us off course. And to take it a step farther:

SO WE FIX OUR EYES NOT ON WHAT IS SEEN, BUT ON WHAT IS UNSEEN, SINCE WHAT IS SEEN IS TEMPORARY, BUT WHAT IS UNSEEN IS ETERNAL.

— 2 Corinthians 4:18 NIV
(EMPHASIS ADDED)

Wait. Now we have to focus on things that we can't even see? How much harder can this get? Well, I guess that's dependent on the strength of our beliefs.

Remember when I said to start with the Person before the place? This is exactly why. If our trust is in Jesus *(Person)*, then where we need to focus is on Him. Meaning, He holds the responsibility for where we end up. Our responsibility is whether or not we listen and go.

All of this may seem like a lot to take in for just our first installment of the faith part of the F.O.C.U.S. method, but remember this does not have to be an all-at-once read. I would love nothing more than to learn that this book has become something you regularly return to for encouragement and reminders. So continue on VAL, grace by grace, one step at a time. I'm right there with ya, friend.

FAITH F.*O*.C.U.S.

O is for obeying.

Once we have fixed our eyes by way of focusing our thoughts on and in Jesus, the next step can either be fun or grueling. "Obedience" is rarely a word that brings warm and fuzzy feelings, yet our greatest rewards can be found on the other side of this prickly noun, obedience.

Maybe we have such a bad relationship with this word because it's about complying with an order, request, law, or another's authority. "That sounds fun!" said no one ever when we think of being under someone's authority. We prefer to want to do things our own way.

However, much of our everyday life falls into the category of obedience, whether we like it or not. Do you pay taxes? Do you purchase things or just take them as needed? Drive a vehicle? What do you do in and with that vehicle? Of course, we don't always obey. Right now, I can think of rules that I don't always follow; the speed limit is one that pops immediately to mind. How about you?

While we could go back and forth at length about things we agree and disagree with when it comes to everyday obedience, there's a different perspective I'd like to shift our focus toward. When it comes to obedience *of the biblical kind*, we tend to want to resist. This is particularly true the moment we feel we've done something warranting God's disapproval, according to ... who exactly? A preacher, Christian friend, the world's moral compass?

In any case, we tend to imagine God looking down on us with a scowl on His face, arms crossed, foot-tapping.

Yet, that could not be further from the actual truth!

Biblical obedience is about *love*. Okay, so maybe you know this or can appreciate this concept, but maybe not enough to fully take it to heart. I get it and can understand based on all that we see, hear, and even have been taught when it comes to biblical obedience. Love is not exactly the first thought that comes to mind for me, either.

We're usually handed one of two scenarios:

1. Do this or else ____ *(a bad thing will happen)*
2. Do this and ____ *(a good thing will result).*

Yet the kind of obedience that God seeks from us stems directly from His love for us. He loves us enough to put up parameters, boundaries, and safety nets. And when we love Him enough to trust that He established them for our good, we'll find obedience to them quite beneficial. (Does the puzzle framework come to mind at all?)

THERE'S A BIGGER PICTURE.

The Old Testament book of Deuteronomy is one of the places I turn to be reminded of the lengths God will go to show His love for His people and what's promised to those who follow His parameters, boundaries, and safety nets. But I realize others may not recognize this because they get too hung up on biblical words like "laws," "commands," or "decrees." I know I can and still do at times.

HEAR, ISRAEL, AND BE
CAREFUL TO OBEY SO
THAT IT MAY GO WELL
WITH YOU AND THAT
YOU MAY INCREASE
GREATLY IN A LAND
FLOWING WITH MILK
AND HONEY, JUST AS
THE LORD, THE GOD
OF YOUR ANCESTORS,
PROMISED YOU.

- Deuteronomy 6:3 NIV
(EMPHASIS ADDED)

Deuteronomy was written by Moses—you know, the guy who was given the Ten Commandments and who led the Israelites out of captivity, through the parted waters of the Red Sea, and wandered around with them in the wilderness listening to them complain for forty years. Yet despite *all that*, he was not allowed to enter the Promised Land that he had spent forty years leading them to! Why? Because of his own disobedience.

Talk about moving past your emotions for the bigger picture. The book of Deuteronomy, which means "second law," is Moses's final plea to the people to get their acts together. If the whole Bible is God's love letter to us, Deuteronomy is Moses's final appeal and reminder to the people he was assigned to lead.

The part to pay attention to here is, "*be careful to obey* so that it may go well with you" (emphasis added). In order to *be careful*, one must be thoughtful, intentional, and purposeful. *To obey* is to do what is asked of you by someone who holds a position of authority or someone you trust and respect. Why? Well, in this example and in God's plan of accomplishing things, it's *so that it may go well with you*. Ah, that part really packs a punch, doesn't it?

I can hear you asking me, "If God is so good, why do bad things happen?" I get asked this question a lot, and I understand the sentiment behind it. The best answer I can give you is that when bad things happen, we want to lay blame somewhere. Someone needs to be responsible, right? Well, God is the biggest authority that we know, so it would seem to make sense that the buck stops with Him. That's exactly where many people look and direct the blame.

IN FACT, THIS IS LOVE FOR GOD: TO KEEP HIS COMMANDS. AND HIS COMMANDS ARE NOT BURDENSOME, FOR EVERYONE BORN OF GOD OVERCOMES THE WORLD. THIS IS THE VICTORY THAT HAS OVERCOME THE WORLD, EVEN OUR FAITH. WHO IS IT THAT OVERCOMES THE WORLD? ONLY THE ONE WHO BELIEVES THAT JESUS IS THE SON OF GOD.

- 1 John 5:3-5 NIV

While not everything can be traced back to a specific conse-quence of disobedience, there are plenty of things that can be. Like getting a ticket for a traffic violation, being injured because you chose not to follow safety guidelines, or ending or losing a relationship because boundaries were crossed, just to name a few.

The following are the exact notes that I have written in my Bible above, below, and next to 1 John 5:3-5 after wrestling with under-standing "if God is so good, why do bad things happen?" for myself.

> **MY NOTES:** *This passage makes me think of all the "complaints" of the world and … "If God is so good—why do bad things happen?" It's lack of love from one another—it's our fault, not God's. His love should be radiating through us. If we don't love Him and obey His Word, we have "no good" to show for it! And next to the last part of verse 3 … His commands are not burdensome … I have written, think of how hard it is to be/remain, rebellious, vengeful, unforgiving, etc.*

Can you trace one of your *"bad things"* back to being the result of not doing something that God directed you to do? Maybe the outcome or event itself wasn't necessarily "bad," but maybe it involved delays or frustrations. There have been a lot of shiny objects I pursued in my business that did not work out very well over the years. I chose shiny trends, gurus, and products over what I knew God actually wanted me to work on. Remember how hard it was for me to let go of my "good thing" for God's better back in Chapter 1? I could use this book as an example of one of those things I procrastinated obeying for various reasons, but S.O.S. (Chapter 6) would be what it ultimately boiled down to.

I've heard it said that if you're not making forward progress, then you should go back and do the last thing that required your obedience to God. Yes, that's tough and definitely humbling, but I've certainly found it to be true.

FAITH F.O.*C*.U.S.
C is for Confess.

This part of the faith F.O.**C**.U.S. method is about as comfy to cover as our last word was. While confession tends to bring to mind the things we feel guilty about, it's actually not as bad as we often make it out to be. Well, I guess that depends on how you felt about its friend, obedience.

We like options. Confession is as optional as obedience, but the relief it brings tends to happen quicker. When we are obedient to something, we don't always see the immediate results.

> *If we confess our sins, he is faithful and just and will forgive us our sins and purify us from all unrighteousness.*
> **- 1 JOHN 1:9 NIV**
> *(emphasis added)*

When *we confess our sins,* a shift in power happens. But before we talk about that, let's first be sure you don't get too hung up on or dismiss this important concept because of a few words. Specifically, the words "confess" and "sins."

Word Nerd Alert

LET'S BETTER UNDERSTAND → CONFESS

In the original Greek, the word "confess" is *homologeo*[1] and its meanings include:

- to say the same thing as another (i.e., to agree with; assent)
- to concede
- not to refuse, to promise
- not to deny
- to confess (i.e., to admit or declare one's self guilty of what one is accused of)
- to profess
- to declare openly, speak out freely

LET'S BETTER UNDERSTAND → SIN

The original Greek word for "sin" is *hamartia*[2] and its meanings include:

- to be without a share in
- to miss the mark
- to err, be mistaken
- to miss or wander from the path of uprightness and honor, to do or go wrong
- to wander from the law of God, violate God's law, sin

---

1 https://www.blueletterbible.org/lexicon/g3670/kjv/tr/0-1/

2 https://www.blueletterbible.org/lexicon/g266/kjv/tr/0-1/

Where sin once had you missing the mark, wandering, doing, or going wrong, confession brings release from the hold sin had over us. The best part of this verse is what happens *after* we do our part.

> *If we confess our sins (our part), He will: forgive us our sins (our missed marks) and purify (cleanse) us from all unrighteousness (injustice).*

In other words, once we confess, we no longer have to live in denial or hide; we can once again live freely out in the open.

Fixing, **O**beying, and **C**onfessing are all individual responsibilities. They require serious inward work, but when you put in that work, you'll see the outward results.

Whew! Do you need a minute? I know this is a lot, either because you may be hearing this for the first time or from a new perspective. Wait 'til you see what comes next!

F.O.C.**U**.S.
U is for United.

We recognize history as past events. However, with our moment-by-moment access to what's happening on the world's stage, we can practically see history in the making. How long did it take you to realize that the global pandemic of 2020 was of historic proportions? And that you were a part of that history? Whether willingly, knowingly, or not, you lived through a historic event. Today, the world is more accessible and connected than ever before, yet simultaneously polarized and disconnected. It's truly a fascinating phenomenon.

SLOGANS, BATTLECRIES, AND MANTRAS-OH, MY!

"We have to be united." We have heard—and still hear—this slogan from every side of the invisible-but-very-much-there fence. It has become the battle cry of our present culture and anyone found on the undesirable or unpopular side of this unity fence is made to feel "wrong."

What's interesting is how adamant "both sides" are on the correct definition, approach, and plan to get to the desired goal of unity.

Well, here's the kicker, VAL ... unity is a result, not a goal. To be of one mind and in agreement with others is a result of something much bigger and greater than us: love.

I'll wait while you let that one sink in. Replay all of the mantras, slogans, cries, and directives you've heard when it comes to uniting, whether in our own or another country. Now consider God's Word:

We can take the word of others about how to "get unified" or we can take God at His Word. The next time you're feeling coerced, pressured, or directed to do something, first be sure it lines up with what God says. *There is no one or nothing that loves you more than He does.* Can you just imagine the progress we could make if we were all unified on that?!

And for the record, before you go looking for my email, I'll save you the effort. My goal is to love you no matter what side of the "get unified" fence you're on. That's the thing about love. We can be in full agreement or adamantly opposed about things *while simultaneously loving and respecting each other.* And yes, that often takes some divine intervention, but it's absolutely possible. So if you're wondering which "side" I'm on, it's the one that agrees with the truth that we are both loved by God and nothing will change that, no matter what.

Without love, unity just isn't possible. (and yes, you can still love while having boundaries, remember Chapter 5?)

F.O.C.U.*S*.
S is for Stand Firm!

Throughout this book, and especially in these last few sections, we've pretty much belabored the point that we act what we believe. Well, I guess you could say that this is where the rubber meets the road, my friend.

There's an old saying that states, "Either stand firm for something or you'll fall for anything." What does it even look like to stand firm?

SEE TO IT THAT
NO ONE TAKES
YOU CAPTIVE
THROUGH HOLLOW
AND DECEPTIVE
PHILOSOPHY,
WHICH DEPENDS
ON HUMAN
TRADITION AND
THE ELEMENTAL
SPIRITUAL FORCES
OF THIS WORLD
RATHER THAN ON
CHRIST.

– *Colossians 2:8 NIV*

Let's think about it literally. First, you put your feet about shoulder-width apart or maybe one foot slightly in front of the other. You bend your knees slightly and lean forward just a smidge. In this stance, you feel centered and ready. You're standing firm.

Centered and ready. When was the last time your priorities reflected that sentiment? How about your focus? Well, without defined and protected priorities, focus is just a fleeting pursuit. To avoid being caught off guard, prepare a reflective response to those questions.

Do you know what it is you stand for, VAL? Even more than that, do you know who it is God has asked you to stand in the gap for?

I looked for someone among them who would build up the wall and stand before me in the gap on behalf of the land so I would not have to destroy it, but I found no one.

- EZEKIEL 22:30 NIV

Let's not end up experiencing the same fate as the people in the land God had to destroy because of all of the evil going on in it. How sad is that, by the way? In an entire country, *not one person* was found to stand in the gap on behalf of its citizens. We have got to get our stance right.

I feel like we are watching this being played out before us today. When can people be found standing firm in the gap for others?

- When it's convenient, sure.
- When it aligns with the narrative that's popular, yup.
- When there's much to gain and little to lose, you betcha.
- How about when no one is watching?

I, for one, do not want to be caught off guard when it comes to standing in the gap for who I've been assigned. Do you?

All the money, influence, achievements, and whatever else you deem as successful in the world's view will not matter one bit if you trade it for your God-given dream and purpose through Christ.

What will it take for you to stand firm in your faith? Only you can answer that question. I have no formula, quick tips, or cute quips. (Sorry to disappoint!) What I *can* tell you that while there may be no shortcuts for the work and processes needed, God has and uses some amazing accelerators! But you'll have to F.O.C.U.S.:

What good is it for someone to gain the whole world, yet forfeit their soul?

- MARK 8:36 NIV

Fix your faith when you need to,
Obey what is revealed,
Confess what has you missing the mark, so that you can
Unify with Him and others through love to be balanced and ready to
Stand firm in what He's said, asked of you, and for who's He's assigned you!

Congratulations! You just completed part one of the three-part F.O.C.U.S. method. And honestly, if you get this one right, as well as the methods that apply to your life and business/work, then you'll be well on your way to serious, prioritized focus.

OBSTACLES ARE
THOSE FRIGHTFUL
THINGS THAT YOU
SEE WHEN YOU
TAKE YOUR EYE
OFF YOUR GOAL.

— Henry Ford

CHAPTER 11

Life F.O.C.U.S.

FINDING YOUR PRIORITIES
IN DAILY LIVING

DO YOUR DAILY PLANS OFTEN FALL SHORT OF YOUR EXPECTATIONS? Mine do, too! As goal-getters it can be hard to separate the big, someday dream from the plans and strategies needed for your day-to-day progress. While there are often things that come up that are beyond your control, it's important to remember the things that you *can* change.

The goal of this chapter, Life F.O.C.U.S., is to give you some guidance and a way to assess where you are while staying on course for where it is you need to go. I encourage you to tweak and customize the method for your own best progress!

LIFE $\mathcal{F}$.O.C.U.S.
F is for Feasible

Think of your next goal (big or small), determine where it fits when it comes to your 4 Frustrating F's (refer back to Chapter 5), and ask yourself, "Is this even feasible right now in this season of my life?" Consider the current pace at which you're working it and the other responsibilities already on your plate. Things like a vacation, a scheduled work deadline, or upcoming celebration (wedding, birthday, etc.).

Now, since we are focusing on the in-front-of-you goals in this chapter, think of goals that are no more than 30–90 days out. As it relates to those goals (but still within one of your 4 F's), list the things you'll *have to* accomplish, as well as the things you *want to do* in order to achieve them.

Take a minute and write them out. At the top of one side of your paper, write "HAVE TO" and on the other side, write "WANT TO." Ahh, you are getting to know me well—I've simplified it for you by providing the columns here for your convenience. Give it a try:

FEASIBILITY FACTOR
TEST #1

HAVE TO

WANT TO

Which side is longer? I know for me, one side will tend to be longer than the other, depending on the type of goal, which reveals if I'm refraining from being *real*. Did you see that in yourself, too?

For example, if I have a particular financial goal, my "want to" side will typically be longer than my "have to" side. That's okay; the process can be messy. But it gets easier with awareness and practice—and a messy process doesn't mean the results will be! Keep going.

FEASIBILITY FACTOR TEST #2

Look at your answers on your "want to" side. How important are they? Prove it by putting them in order of priority. Don't stress over this too much. The easiest way to accomplish this is to give them each a timeframe. Let's be a bit more specific than now, later, or someday, shall we? I'm encouraging you to get more granular— this month, the next 90 days, this year, five, ten years, and so forth. See? I'm here to help!

FEASIBILITY FACTOR TEST #3

How many of the "have tos" can be automated, delegated, or elim-inated? This one should just take a few seconds. Mark an "A" for automate, "D" for delegate, and "E" for eliminate.

Automated is pretty self-explanatory and often includes bill payments, renewals, and things like that. Delegated means that a particular to-do item could be *done for you*. Think carpool, cook, clean, shop, admin stuff, schedule your social media posts, etcetera. The final and toughest of the three options is to eliminate. Why is this one so tough? Because we can't seem to come to grips *or admit* that we need to let some things go. Our to-do lists are our claim to fame! I'll lose my badge of honor! (Insert eye roll here.) One tip that might help you overcome this tough one is to remember that it doesn't mean you have to eliminate it forever.

Well, what did your feasibility tests reveal about your commitment to your goals? It's not that your goals aren't feasible, just maybe your expected timeframes to achieve them need to be adjusted. Life F.O.C.U.S. begins with feasibility. Now that you know how to determine if you're being honest with yourself about your goals as it relates to your day-to-day reality, you're ready to move on to the next step.

LIFE F.*O*.C.U.S

O is for Optimizing

Optimize is a verb that essentially means *to make the best or most effective use of a situation, opportunity, or resource.* That includes your goals.

Once you determine what's realistic (i.e., feasible) and set your sights on making that happen, it's time to work on optimizing your potential outcome! Remember, we cannot control outcomes, but we sure can influence them based on our output.

The most important thing to remember about optimizing outcomes is your willingness. Before you're motivated to act, you first need to be inspired. Inspiration is an inside job; one where *only you* can fuel the spark that ignites motivation. In order to set yourself up for the best possible outcome, you need to identify what inspires you about your goal and then keep it in front of you. I would even write it down.

Motivation is an outward result of inward inspiration.

There are too many goal-setters out there going after the *wrong goal*! And sadly, they never graduate from goal-setter to goal-getter. I don't want you to be one of them. So ask yourself: "What am I willing to do in order to achieve my goal?" We're great at to-do lists. But what about what *not* to do in order to achieve your goal?

I'm going to have you make another list. (Don't roll your eyes.) This time, create two columns labeled "To-Do" and "To-Don't." Believe it or not, this simple step packs a potent punch when making progress toward your goal.

I'll give you an example before you jump to filling out your lists, but know that optimizing your chances of success should be *fun*!

Let's say one of your goals is to drink more water (this happens to be one of my personal goals, too). But that's so vague and boring. How can you optimize this goal and make it more specific and fun? Instead of saying your goal is to drink "more" water, how much more? Give it a specific amount. What's the timeframe? Do you need to have all your ounces consumed well before bedtime so you're not up all night going to the bathroom? Put a time on it. Or better yet, break it down into several timeframes by ounces.

As for how you can make it more fun, consider using my method: To ensure I consume my daily ounce goal by six o'clock in the evening, I use inspiring cups and fun, colored straws throughout the day. My middle child carries a sixty-four-ounce, hot pink stainless-steel thermos with a "sippy lid" (as I call it). It goes wherever she goes like it's her blanky—and she's in college! It's just as worn out as you would imagine a childhood blanket would be, too, with dents, chips, and the color faded. The point is: Do what works for you. Don't be afraid to experiment with it; have fun and stretch yourself!

Back to the optimization list and our example. Your to-do item is drinking more water. A to-don't item might be to not drink anything with sugar in it. A to-do: place an eight-ounce glass full of water on your nightstand before bed while a to-don't would be to not stand up from bed in the morning until you drank it! See how you can make specific and actionable to-do and to-don't items for your goal-getting list?

Now it's your turn to start putting this into action. Now that you're clear on a goal and where it falls in helping you improve any of the 4 Frustrating Fs in your list, and you've confirmed that it's feasible now, it's time to fill in the boxes as it relates to your to-do and to-dont's for *that* goal.

OPTIMIZE THAT GOAL!

TO-DO **TO-DON'T**

Now that you've seen how this works, I hope that you'll make it a regular practice whenever you plan your next goal! I think that you'll find optimizing your outcome a fun part of your F.O.C.U.S. method.

SUCCESS TAKES HOW LONG?

While determining the feasibility of your goal can be a bit of work, and optimizing your outcome can be fun, this next part takes some practice and patience.

LIFE F.O.*C*.U.S.

C is for Consistency

We don't gain ten pounds overnight, yet we sure do want it to come off that quickly! Can I tell you a *big* secret? One that will hopefully give you the perspective shift that could change the way you look at any goal?

We've actually talked about this before, but I think this is where it might really hit home!

CONCENTRATE LESS ON THE THINGS THAT YOU NEED TO DO AND FOCUS MORE ON THE PERSON YOU NEED TO BECOME IN ORDER TO HANDLE "THE GOAL."

While discipline is very important when it comes to our goal-getting endeavors, it's our mindset *and attitude* that will support our attempts.

We would rather make lists, charts, trackers, or anything else than decide who we need to be in order to achieve "that goal." But those aren't the things that change you; those are just the things that help you track and make progress. See the difference?

It's kind of like learning another language. You have to first translate the words to yourself, often sounding them out in your mind before you actually speak them out loud. It's said that those who become fluent in another language are able to process the words they want to say more quickly. This is because they can now *think in that language.*

How about you? Are you thinking like the person who has already achieved the goal you're currently working toward? If I want to *be* a writer, I have to think, act, and plan like someone who *is* a writer. If I want to be fit, I have to think, act, and plan like someone who *is* fit. If I want to be bold in sharing my faith, I have to think, act, and speak up like someone who *is* bold in their faith.

Think of any of the goals that you have been working toward, big or small. Even take it a step further and think about where you want to be in your life a year from now, three years, five ....

MINDSET EXCERCISE

WHO DO YOU NEED TO BE AND THINK LIKE *now* IN ORDER TO *become* THAT PERSON LATER? How can you give her some encouragement, guidance, and hope that she can do this? Below are some starter thoughts to get you thinking about what you would say to her.

- You are _____ (encouragement) and I am telling you that you need _____ and I know this because *now* I am _____.
- Take the time to write her a letter.
- Consider putting together a vision board.

Once you begin thinking like that person, you'll start acting like that person. You'll plan, prepare, and make serious progress in *becoming her.*

The best part is that you'll actually be more consistent. Want to know why? Because you want to be known as that person. If you start doing things out of alignment with what is required to become like her, you'll feel like you let her down. Old people-pleasing habits die hard, but in this case, it's in a good way. Don't let *your future self* down!

FUN FACT

The more you familiarize yourself with the VAL (Valued, Amazing Lady, remember?) you want to become, the more your brain will work to protect her, point out opportunities to become like her, and filter what's for or against her. It's really fascinating! Be sure to only accept traits, attributes, and characteristics of her that God says she is. Revisit that chart from Ephesians 1 back in Chapter 3 and then put on that "outfit" and see if that doesn't help you walk, talk, and think more like her.

The key to consistency is determining if you are willing to take on the character of your future self and continually show up as her.

Living a life of F.O.C.U.S must always include the willingness to change and the consistency to create the kind of change that lasts. Consistency isn't easy, but it's doable and worth it. Speaking of not easy, the next part of your life's F.O.C.U.S. is about handling the naysayers, both real and imagined.

LIFE F.O.C.*U*.S.
U is for Unbothered.

Raise your hand if you've ever felt crushed as a result of what someone has said. Not just about you, but maybe your situation, your loved ones, your project, or a goal that you're working on. Girl, I see you. Keep your hand raised if you've been hurt by the things you *think* they've said. Yep, me, too; both hands are up over on this side of the page, VAL. But know this: *Despite how we're treated, how we treat ourselves, or how we feel, we are still—and always will be—Valued, Amazing Ladies.* I hadn't reminded you of that in this chapter yet, so I felt this was the spot to do it!

Let's just establish the fact that you're in good company. Most of us worry about the things that others think and say about us or do to us. While this is the norm for us, it would be wise to have some type of a go-to plan to combat this emotional and even physical (have you ever been paralyzed by fear?) cycle of being bothered by potential naysayers.

In my experience, an effective way to defeat the naysayers and remain unbothered by them is to embrace your middle-man. Before we get to what that is and how it works, let's talk about why we even have naysayers in the first place.

You see, when we are bothered by a naysayer, it's typically because of one of the following scenarios. See if it's true for you, too. The bothersome, get-under-your-skin-and-in-your-head naysayers usually:

    A. don't understand us, our work, or our goal,
    B. feel unqualified or inferior to us, and/or
    C. thrive on putting others down to feel better about themselves.

NAYSAYER A

Let's look at "Naysayer A." This is the person who has a complete lack of understanding about our work, project, goal, etcetera.

But here's the thing about Naysayer A and why we can't get too upset with them: If *you* don't fully understand what it is you are trying to achieve, how can you expect them to? (Uh-oh; your stuck symptom is showing! See Chapter 5.)

So first and foremost, get clarity on your own goal(s), project, and work. You should be able to explain it to a twelve-year-old. If you can't, it's a big indicator that you may not be all that sure of what you're pursuing and why. (Perhaps take a review lap around Chapters 5–8 real quick.)

Our goals often become our own little world. While so much of the language, logos, lingos, and legends are obvious to us, we have to remember that this is not the case for those who are not a part of that world.

So the next time you find yourself fumbling to answer the question, "What is it you're doing, again?" attempt to explain it to them in a way that would be universally understandable.

Once you're able to share with better clarity and understanding, they will make the connection for you. They may even blurt out, "Oh! Like ___!" And at that point, you'll either nod in agreement or recognize that no amount of explaining and examples will help them understand just what it is that you're trying to achieve. It's time to realize that they're not part of your assigned peeps or in the running for potential partnerships (see Chapter 8). Just smile and move on.

NAYSAYER B

The second type of naysayer (Naysayer B), is often the one in your head, which, by the way, is often the hardest to overcome. However, victory is absolutely possible. The most important thing to remember about this naysaying underminer is that she is driven by feelings.

Feelings follow choice. Feelings are emotional, and emotions are indicators of a deeper issue. Once you find the root of that issue, you have to make a decision, which then leads to directions (see Chapter 3).

> *You can choose to allow the feeling to fester and affect your progress or choose to deal with the root and make progress.*

Be the middle-VAL

Now would be a good time to explain what I mean by middle-man. This concept is simply an easy way to remember that you should always strive to find yourself in the middle. As in, you're not the best, but you're also not the worst. There is someone that is ahead of you and someone else who is behind where you are. You ask for help as well as give it.

THIS IS WHAT
THE LORD SAYS:
"STAND AT THE
CROSSROADS
AND LOOK; ASK
FOR THE ANCIENT
PATHS, ASK WHERE
THE GOOD WAY
IS, AND WALK IN
IT, AND YOU WILL
FIND REST FOR
YOUR SOULS. BUT
YOU SAID, 'WE WILL
NOT WALK IN IT.'"

– Jeremiah 6:16 NIV

This is a great reminder verse. When our souls need rest, what better rest is there than following God's guidance? But the verse also calls out those who don't seek or follow Him; how embarrassing.

I use this verse to point out that there is always someone ahead of you in life that has "been down this road" that you're currently navigating. They can provide helpful guidance if you are brave enough to ask. And as believers, God is always ahead of us, waiting on us to ask for His guidance.

It's important to remember that the "ancient paths" we've been down can be a struggle for someone else currently going down that path. So don't think it odd when they ask which way is the "good way."

Our goal, then, should be to remain connected both with someone ahead of us and another who is just behind us. Hence, us being in the middle. The middle-man. VAL in the middle. Middle-VAL ....

I like to think of it as someone holding my hand through a new or unfamiliar process; one that I'm either looking to improve or need to just get through while in survival mode. At the same time, I'm holding the hand of someone else who's navigating something new, difficult, or unfamiliar. I'm able to comfortably guide them through where I've already been.

Think of this as having a mentor while simultaneously mentoring someone else. *"Stand at the crossroads and look; ask for the ancient paths, ask where the good way is ...."* As Christians, dare I suggest or even imply that this is what discipleship looks like?

NAYSAYER C

The last type of naysayer is one that you should learn to recognize quickly and just as fast, distance yourself! This is the one who does nothing but put down what you're doing, what you're trying to do, and even what you've done.

Why do they do this? Perhaps to make themselves *feel* superior, better, and further ahead; who knows what their end game really is?

All you need to know and remember about this type of naysayer is that they've made no room for you, so bless and release them and keep on moving, sis. They've given you your clue and cue to not only be unbothered by them, but also, to not bother going out of your way to be with them.

The importance of understanding all of these types of naysayers is so you don't end up like or with them! Remember, your goal is to end up in the middle, unbothered by what others think, say, or do *in their attempt to hinder your progress.* That last part is key. You have to be able to differentiate between flagrant naysayers who *intend* to inflict harm and people who offer constructive criticism that you *interpret* as a personal attack on you or your goals.

VAL, take some time to consider who's been where you are now. How did they overcome the obstacles that you're facing currently? What example did they leave for you? Hold that hand.

Who do you know that is struggling in a place that you've already overcome? What help are you giving them? Hold that hand.

Now that you've defined what's feasible, optimized your potential outcome, and are equipped to not only leave the naysayers in the dust, it's time to make sure that you stay on track.

LIFE F.O.C.U.S.
S is for Staying on course and remaining Steady

Staying on course is much easier when you've identified just what your course is! But even more important is to be aware of *where* your course is at all times. Sounds silly, I know, but think of how often—and how far—we find ourselves *off course*.

One of the biggest keys to staying on course is acknowledging that it has little to do with speed. Isn't that interesting?

I don't know about you, but when I think of staying on course, it conjures up visions of a racecourse. And in my mind, racecourse automatically translates to speed—as in fast. So, course = fast. Everything needs to be fast.

Do you struggle with the speed at which you achieve your goals, too? My typical goal scenario will go something like this:

> **STEP 1**—Decide on a goal.
> **STEP 2**—Determine a ridiculously quick timeframe in which said goal is to be achieved.
> **STEP 3**—Don't be in a hurry until that ridiculous "deadline" looms.

So, am I alone in going straight from ready-to-race mode the moment I hear someone say, "stay the course"? I didn't think so.

Here's what I did to help change the narrative from "stay the course" to *remain steady*. Ah, doesn't that already calm the "go" in goal a bit?

3 WAYS TO FOCUS ON REMAINING STEADY

#1 PACE IS MORE IMPORTANT THAN RACE.

Hallelujah! Meaning, *intentional progress is better than the speed at which I make that progress.*

#2 IMPROVEMENT BEGINS AND ENDS WITH ME.

I'm the "IM" in improvement. There can be *no improvement without movement.* You may not have to race, but you do have to move!

#3 EXCHANGE "THE GOAL" FOR MEMORABLE MILESTONES.

Find ways to make note of your progress. This helps with keeping the focus on what's in front of you and gives you something to look forward to!

There will absolutely be seasons when you will feel compelled to run and others when you're barely able to crawl. But then, VAL, there will be times when you feel like you're cruising with the windows down and the music blaring! Either way, keep going because you'll be making progress!

If "Stay the Course" has you racing and pushing too hard, exchange that for "Remaining Steady."

Now that you have part two of the three-part F.O.C.U.S. method, how are you feeling? I'm hoping that you are feeling encouraged but also informed and inspired to take action and make progress toward your goals. Understanding and practicing the Life F.O.C.U.S. method will have you making better decisions about your priorities and the pace at which you execute them in your everyday life.

RECAP

F is for determining what's **FEASIBLE**.

O is for **OPTIMIZING** your goal's outcome.

C is for **CONSISTENCY** in becoming the future you.

U is for embracing your middle-man to be **UNBOTHERED** by naysayers.

S is for **STAYING** the course while remaining **STEADY**.

Let's keep going!

IF YOU DID NOT GET
WHAT YOU WANT,
IT'S EITHER A SIGN
THAT YOU DID NOT
SERIOUSLY WANT
IT, OR THAT YOU
TRIED TO BARGAIN
OVER THE PRICE.

- Rudyard Kipling

CHAPTER 12

Business F.O.C.U.S.

IT'S MORE THAN
PLANS & STRATEGIES

IT'S TIME TO DIG INTO THE THIRD AND FINAL ROUND
OF F.O.C.U.S. ARE YOU READY? Now it's time to dig into
what kind of F.O.C.U.S. you need when it comes to your work,
ministry, or business.

As we discussed way back in Chapter 3, who you are is more
than your role, your titles, or what you do. For some of us, that is a
complicated identity crisis to get past, especially if you fall somewhere on the 'preneur spectrum: solopreneur, semipreneur, or the
most familiar—entrepreneur.

HARMONY OVER BALANCE

Creating the harmony you desire in your faith, your life, and your business takes prioritized focus. And in order to keep those areas harmoniously intersecting, you must learn to keep first things first and know what is non-negotiable.

And yes, I prefer the term harmony over balance any day of the week. Balance has me imagining myself standing at the center of a see-saw while holding spinning plates. I don't know about you, but it doesn't have me drumming up thoughts of, "Hey, I want to live like that!"

What do you imagine when you hear the word "balance?" Do you think in terms of having all accounts zeroed out, as if every area of your life were like a bank account and the currency is your time? How "balanced" are your accounts? Is what you're envisioning a pretty picture, or not so much?

Harmony seems a more realistic vision when we think of the place where our faith, our life, and our business come together. To me, it even sounds better.

GOT IT! NEXT. . .

Just like the two previous chapters, we will be breaking down F.O.C.U.S. step by step here, too. This installment, though, will be centered more on strategy than mindset.

Now before we jump in, there are a few reminders I want to call to your attention about plans and strategies (review Chapter 7, if need be). Remember that a plan has to do with the tools that you need and a strategy is the measurable activities toward your goal. It is also important to note that a plan and a strategy are most effective when you begin with an established dream/vision, mission, and core values.

We've covered these things, but it's important to reiterate so that you don't end up disappointed.

- There is no magic bullet.
- Inner work is crucial and must be done first before any outward work has a chance for success.
- You're ultimately responsible for the success of your goals and your business.

The bottom line is that you are not only encouraged to find what works, but to also tweak other parts to suit you. Keep experimenting until you get the formula that works for you!

Finally, be sure that what you're reading, learning, and who you're learning from falls into that middle-man category from the last chapter. Sometimes we get too far ahead of ourselves that the material we're so anxious to "jump to" is not helpful at all.

It's a "tough love" reminder for me as well as you. I've spent thousands of hours *and* dollars over the years trying to jump into a spot that I was not ready for. Not only was I not ready, but I hadn't even put in the work to prepare for it! It's so much better when you can easily flow from one step to the next. To that end, let's get started with what that could look like for you.

FINDING YOUR FLOW

Imagine what your ideal workweek would look like as your *future* self. Remember we talked about her in the last chapter—she was the "C" for consistency in your Life F.O.C.U.S. method. Think like her.

- How many hours a day do you work?
- How many days a week?
- What does your office look like—do you have an office?
- Who are you serving?
- Are you serving your clients in person, virtually, with physical products, through a service, etcetera?
- What do you typically wear to work—whatever you want or a dress code?

Have you ever given any real thought to these questions? I mean serious thought, as in it's actually a part of your plan *and* strategy to become your reality.

Most of us can imagine with clarity and excitement what we want our businesses to look like. But for some reason, we stop short of *working* toward that vision.

Why is that? Is it because we are more desperate to be seen and known as a success rather than work toward becoming it? Time and time again we sacrifice what we really want in the end for what's in front of us at the moment.

Having a business, being in business, and growing a business is not for the faint of heart. What we actually *do* shows how much we mean business when it comes to our envisioned success and becoming the person who handles it.

Helpful tip: Go back to Chapter 3 and adapt the core values exercise to define your business's core values. Narrow them all the way down to the 3–5 things you want your business to be known for. These core values will help you filter decisions for your business!

IN YOUR BUSINESS

Ah, working *in* your business versus working *on* your business— that's where the wantrepreneurs are separated from the entrepreneurs. Not sure where you're camped right now?

Think of working *in* your business as how your business *appears*. Working *on* your business utilizes the strategies and projects that result in you *producing and improving.* So to really simplify it, *in* = appearance and *on* = production.

You certainly need both aspects. Yes, people need to know where to find you, what you're about, and what you offer (working *in* your business*).* But you also need to partner, produce, and get paid—things that require you to work *on* your business.

You've defined who you serve and why, discovered what you provide, and determined how you provide that service. Now it's time to do it! Only after you have determined where and when that happens can you hope to amplify your impact, income, and influence. This is what I like to call your flow.

THE FLOW TO GROW

Here is another sticky (albeit a bit corny) way to help remember how amplifying your impact, income, and influence actually works.

FLOW + GLOW = GROWTH

YOUR FLOW → That God-given "thing" He has especially equipped and assigned you to do in service *for others*. When you're not overthinking or overcomplicating it, it's easy for you. You are even surprised to hear that it's so special or unique.

YOUR GLOW → Everyone can see when you're in your sweet spot. What you or others may not recognize is that it's literally your face reflecting God's gift *to you* for the sake of others. People can see how lit up you are about it, are happy for you, and can't help but be sparked by your glow.

THE GROWTH → The result of living in your flow and showing off your glow! The results are felt by others *and* you, benefitting you both.

GO AHEAD AND FIND YOURS

YOUR FLOW

What's the thing, *your thing,* that God has especially equipped and encouraged you to do in service for others?

YOUR GLOW

What's the thing, *your thing*, that all can recognize as your sweet spot? It's literally your face reflecting His gift to you for the sake of others.

THE GROWTH

What are some of the results you have seen when you have lived in your flow, showing off your glow?

This is exactly the type of harmony I'm talking about! Doesn't this equation spark something a lot more inspiring than simply the daunting quest for balance?

I think so and I believe it makes these next F.O.C.U.S. strategies that much more inspiring and motivating to execute.

FINDING YOUR BUSINESS *F*.O.C.U.S.
F is for Follow-Up.

How strong is your follow-up game? I ask because I'm hoping to find myself in the good company of others who are a bit weak in this area, too. I know—I can't believe I just exposed that truth to you about me, either, but alas, I'm often guilty. However, I have improved over the years and have discovered some methods that help in this regard.

Follow-up is a huge part of the success of any endeavor, especially for business. Yet so many of us let it slip through the cracks of our day-to-day, probably because it falls into the working *on* your business category, which most times is less fun than working *in* your business.

TAKING FOLLOW-UP TO TASK

To help you regularly follow-up with clients, create and maintain a running list of who you need to touch base with as well as individuals you just want to get to know better. Be sure to note the reason for each follow-up/contact.

I then plug those names into specific days on my calendar. The follow-up could happen within a few days or even up to a month or more in the future. The *way* I follow up is dependent on our initial connection and/or history; the follow-up could be a text, phone call, email, or—my favorite—"happy mail" (aka snail mail). Oftentimes, it's a mix of these methods.

Another follow-up method that I love, even as a tech-resistant person, is automated email (if you have some type of email opt-in offer or lead magnet). I won't go into too much detail here, but if you have a welcome email sequence, it's a built-in type of follow-up. While that's great for automation, another follow-up method I love to use is snail mail! Sending postcards is a fun way to "show up" in your follow-up! It can also be an effective way to spread the word about your business. You'd better believe those those postcards have my website on them! Whether it's the mail carrier, the recipient, or their colleagues and clients who see it sitting on their desk or counter, the postcard is a way to get more people to learn what my business is about and where to find me.

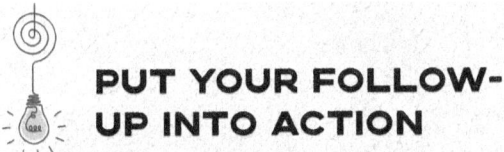

PUT YOUR FOLLOW-UP INTO ACTION

Create a list **WHO** needs follow-up and their connection point.

Note **WHY** the follow-up is needed.

Schedule **WHEN** the follow-up will happen (no matter how soon or far out).

Determine **HOW** that follow-up will happen (the method).

Consider **WHAT** is expected next from each of you.

To quickly sum it up: follow-up has to do with "old business." Meaning, you have already established some type of connection or relationship with this person, organization, or team that you are now following up with. You are literally following up to see what's next. Sometimes "what's next" is scheduling another time to connect, close a sale, make a referral, or discuss a new opportunity. But there's a good chance that none of these things will happen if you don't take the time to create a system that has you regularly following up with existing clients.

BOTTOM LINE. . .

Your follow-up should always be about finding out what *they* want from you next, not what *you* want from them. No one wants to feel like they're being sold to. Yes, you are in business and need to make sales, but give the spotlight to your customer/client.

Your ultimate job is to make sure that they come out the hero. You're just the sidekick that helps them choose the right cape for their mission.

FINDING YOUR BUSINESS F.*O*.C.U.S.

O is for Outreach/Onboarding.

OLD IS GREAT, BUT NEW IS NECESSARY

So if "F" is for following up on old business, then "O" is all about the outreach and onboarding of new business. While it's a good practice to offer new items/services to existing clients and customers, *it's not going to help you grow or bring in new business.*

It's one thing to give an existing customer the inside scoop and first dibs on what's new; it's another to be sure that you're not selling them to death. When I'm sold to death, I can't remove myself fast enough from their emails, private messages, and texts! You don't want that to happen to you.

We entrepreneurs often think we need to continually come up with new *things* in order to keep our existing (old) business engaged and buying, when in reality, we need to focus on regularly sharing our core MESSage with new *people.*

This book is a prime example of my *new* way of sharing my core MESSage. Many of my clients, blog readers, and workshop attendees have heard a lot of this information before. But chances are good that as the reader of this book, you may be new to this "old info" and that's what keeps this VAL inspired, motivated, and moving!

FINDERS KEEPERS!

Where would someone new find you, your business/ministry/ organization, or your service? A website, social media, a product on a store shelf, a referral ...? Think of the welcome mats you lay out for your potential new peeps once they find you. How do you want that new guest to feel upon their first encounter with you and your business?

This is something that *we think* that we've put a lot of thought into, but in reality, we often haven't fully considered *the client's experience.*

TIP TO REMEMBER:

Don't get more caught up in the colors of your site, logo, and products than considering how you want your new guests to feel or what you want them to learn.

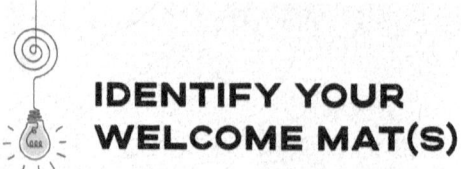

IDENTIFY YOUR WELCOME MAT(S)

WEBSITE
How do they find it?
Blog, social media, ads, event, opt-in …

SOCIAL MEDIA
How do they find it? Is it public or private?
An ad, post, share, group, link …

PRODUCT
How do they find it?
Link on your website, social media, blog, in a virtual or brick-and-mortar store …

OTHER PEOPLE

How are you partnering with others to share your
welcome mats?

Events, shared links/posts, as a guest on their platforms ...

**WHAT CONSISTENT AND EFFECTIVE "OLD"
MESSAGE ARE YOU SHARING WITH *new*
PEOPLE?**

**HOW DO YOU WANT THEM TO *feel* ONCE
THEY'VE DECIDED TO STEP ONTO YOUR
WELCOME MAT?**

ALL ABOARD!

Now that you know how important it is to place their needs and wants before your own, consider your current onboarding process.

Think of a recent experience you have had as a new client of someone else. Take note of what you really liked, how you felt, what turned you off, and what made you want more. Seriously, you should keep a running list of all of these things and then use all of that to create a uniquely positive onboarding experience for your new guests! (I have digital files of pictures and examples of packaging, thank-you postcards, email wording, and anything that I have loved during a new customer experience.)

TAKE ACTION & NOTE

List 3 businesses you LOVE visiting:

Are they virtual or physical?

Why are these your favorites?

What are the feelings you have when you interact
with them?

How can/will you incorporate their techniques into
your own customer/client/guest experience?

DON'T STOP!

Oh, by the way, this strategy is not just about onboarding new
peeps; it's also about outreach. It's awesome to have a system that
seamlessly takes a new guest from welcome to what's next, which
is outreach.

Outreach is about individualizing and making their experience
personal. It could be a welcome postcard in the mail. A private
message after the public welcome on your social media page or
group, or just a quick email to say, "I'm glad you're here!"

The strategy here is to *create a solid, repeatable welcome experience for your new guests.* One that is totally reflective of you, your
personality, and confirms they are, in fact, welcome in your circle
of influence.

While onboarding and outreach help welcome new people, keep in mind that they are still guests at this point. Whether or not they stay and continue on with you depends on your next part of F.O.C.U.S.

FINDING YOUR BUSINESS F.O.*C*.U.S

C is for Content.

In the world of marketing and attracting your assigned peeps, content is king! Remember, your peeps aren't just your audience and they're more than a potential customer; they're who you were assigned to stand in the gap for and help! As the one in charge of your business, it's your job to help them quickly decide if you're a right fit for them.

From the graphics you use to the color scheme you choose, it all points to what you are saying, who you are saying it to, and why. Your brand is how all of that ties together in a distinct and recognizable way that can be traced back to you. You represent your brand, *but it is not your identity* (refer back to Chapter 3).

Get your assignment right and the branding and messaging will flow much easier.

GETTING IT RIGHT.

Your content is *that thing* you are passionate about; the MESSage that you were entrusted to share with those assigned to you. Think of content as your way of showing your flow + your glow *in action*.

When done correctly, your content will attract new and solidify existing members in a way that has them thinking, "How does she know?!" Now, does everything get hit out of the park? No, but consistency does a much better job of attracting the right kind of visibility than that one viral post-thing you keep hoping for. This needs to be said again: Stop trying to hit the grand slam[1] when there's no one on base! Besides, even if you *do* get a grand slam here and there, that's a heck of a welcome, but then what? Are you prepared to back up that hit?

THERE'S ONLY SO MUCH NEW

Content is super important, but *you have to be consistent.* Can I tell you a secret? This one is going to lift a huge weight from you.

Ready? Consistency does not mean you have to constantly create something new. Wait ... what? Yep, you don't always have to create new content.

Just like your onboarding/outreach practice is all about sharing your "old" tried-and-true message with new people, content can be created to fall into that category of practice, too.

REUSE, RECYCLE, AND REPURPOSE

For years, I put pressure on myself to write a new blog post *every week,* and for a while, I was cranking those posts out. Then I got behind and began to panic. If I had no new blog post, I couldn't send out the weekly email. No new blog post also meant no new social media post. Once that seed of defeat started cycling in my mindset, I began feeling stuck!

---

1   A grand slam in the game of baseball is when the bases are loaded and the batter hits a home run, enabling all four of those players to score.

Then I learned about repurposing content. I learned that the focus shouldn't be so much on trying to say something new but on sharing my core message in new ways and with new people.

Repurposed content can be just as fabulous as brand-new content. And here's the thing: Sometimes it's even better!

Think of how many times you have to see a slogan, watch a commercial, or hear a jingle before its message really sticks. For most of us, it takes at least a couple of times.

Too many of us get caught up in thinking that we have to say something *new* all of the time. *That actually confuses people.* Do you know what confused people do? Leave. Say no. Don't leave reviews or give referrals. Unfollow, unsubscribe, quit.

So as you create your content, remember to also present an "old" idea or concept in fresh, new ways.

Think about your core MESSage. Can you categorize that message into different areas, aspects, or perspectives?

For example, my core MESSage centers around ways of finding, keeping, and improving focus. I believe this is important because we were each gifted a dream that God intended for us to share with a specific group of people. Without focus, we will not live up to the vision and mission God created for us! I have chosen to categorize this message into three different areas: our faith, our everyday life, and business. So essentially, each piece of core content that I come up with can be shared from these three perspectives: faith, life, and business.

Your turn! How many different ways and areas can you spread your core MESSage for your business?

Once you get the hang of it, it's kind of fun!

TEST IT OUT

Brainstorm some ways you can present an "old" idea/concept in a fresh new way without changing your core MESSage:

What are the areas, aspects, and perspectives you can use to share your MESSage?

Can you categorize those areas, aspects, or perspectives?

Consistently sharing your core MESSage in new and effective ways means being intentional about *how* you do it (email, social media, blog, podcast, video, etc.) and purposeful about *who* it will attract and why.

Your assignments are waiting on you. Will you be able to guide them along your welcome mats to the core of what you've been entrusted to tell them?

By this point, you may be feeling a bit overwhelmed yet excited enough to want to jump right in and start updating everything related to your business! I get it, so let's get to our next part of F.O.C.U.S.

FINDING YOUR BUSINESS F.O.C.*U*.S.
U is for the Update!

I'll tell you straight out of the gate that "update" includes both personal as well as business activities. So while on the surface the concept of update sounds straightforward, it can be a little tricky.

Consider the feel-good, memorable onboarding experiences from those places you love to go and visit. Got it? Okay, now imagine that the business owner started giving you play-by-play, in-the-moment updates. We all love to feel like we're *in the know,* right? But not when it seems random or disconnected as to why we opted into becoming one of their peeps in the first place.

Sure, both of these types of updates (the in-the-know kind and the play-by-play kind) have their place, but do you know when each is appropriate for your business? Hint: It's based on the goals you have for it.

Take a moment to assess your current communication with your assigned peeps and partners. What have you established with them? How often are you communicating updates? Is it enough, too much, or too little? Does it align with what you said you'd provide when they agreed to receive communications from you? How do you know?

Where does your primary communication take place—via social media, email, texts, or some other method? These are important questions to answer. Once you determine the best type of update, method, and time—stick with them!

You can always throw in extras here and there, but it's important to create a framework and foundation for updates. Whether it's posting three times a week on social media, sending out a weekly e-newsletter, or scheduling a once-a-week text, find what works and resonates best for both you and your peeps ... and then be consistent!

Updates should also include your calendar (both personal and business), lists, follow-ups, onboarding/outreach messages, emails, etcetera. Whether you are keeping track via digital, paper, or big ol' dry-erase style, keep staying up-to-date using a method that works for you *and*—you guessed it—be consistent.

There is no right or wrong way to do your updating as long as you actually implement and *do* it! So experiment, track, create, and tweak ... but take action and be consistent.

I prefer 30-day-at-a-time experiments, which give you a small enough window of time to be consistent, while also giving you some usable data.

FINDING YOUR UPDATE
FOUNDATION & FRAMEWORK

What type(s) of communication have I
established with my peeps & partners?

How often are those updated?

Which are most effective?

How do I know?

Where am I keeping track of my communication for
my personal life and my business?

Is my current system helping me make progress toward my goal?

Are there any improvements I can make? Something new I can try?

The one thing I'm going to experiment with in the next 30 days is:

We've covered a lot of Business F.O.C.U.S. so far: the follow-up, onboarding/outreach, content, consistency, and the importance of the updates. Now it's time for the part we all love to hate—the sale!

FINDING YOUR BUSINESS F.O.C.U.S.
S is for Sales!

You knew that we had to talk about this one at some point, right? We can't have a business if we don't have sales. The sooner you learn how to comfortably share your promotions, offers, services, courses, products, and more, the better your sales will be.

Speaking of better sales, do you know what yours need to be in order to reach your goals? I find it absolutely fascinating how many people have no idea what their sales need to be in order to ___ (their goal). That blank could be anything from having enough money to pay for little Johnny's soccer uniform and travel expenses, to how much you need to have in savings before you can quit your 9–5 and make "this" your full-time business.

WHAT WILL IT TAKE?

Once you have that number, determine how many products/services you need to sell to reach that goal. Then give it a time frame.

The time frame becomes your promotion period that leads up to your launch. Launch simply means you are flipping the business sign to *open*!

Now, whether or not flipping that sign translates to sales depends on a few things: Your messaging to the right people, your offers actually satisfy a need they have, and there's a clear path in how to get what they need from you. They need your specialized roadmap that was designed just for them. And they need it soon after they've landed on your welcome mat.

For us, we could say our roadmap is this current F.O.C.U.S. method we're working through. It has various stops and exits to choose from while on the journey to amplify your business focus. You can choose how much or little you "drive" when it comes to **F**ollow-up, **C**ontent, **U**pdates, and **S**ales.

Aren't roadmaps much easier to handle and follow than wandering and wondering what's next? The same is true for those you've been assigned through your business. Make it easy on them, take care of them, and guide them to the quickest route to the needed solution you've been entrusted to share with them.

THE T.I.E. THAT BINDS

Think back to one of your own buying experiences. What brought you to the store/service/seller? Why did you choose that particular one over another? How many times did you connect with the store/service/seller before you decided to explore their offer?

Odds are good that you're no different than any other buyer out there and went through the following three stages before purchasing:

1. You realized you were in need of some form of a desired transformation (you are here and have this, but want to be there and have that).
2. You began your hunt for information (what you need to know in order to make a decision).
3. You found a few that you were interested in and allowed them to educate you on just how they would deliver the transformation you were seeking.

In other words, you stepped onto their welcome mat and followed their roadmap; it was their T.I.E. between you and their business:

TRANSFORMATION → What relief can your business bring your peeps? Share how you have helped others with the same issue/mess they are currently experiencing? Use testimonials, my friend—they are gold!

INFORMATION → How are you providing the information they need to make a decision? Is it relevant to where they are now? Does it point them to the solution you have for the relief and transformation they want? Are they thinking, "How does she know that about me/my problem?"

EDUCATION → Do you show the solution process from the beginning to the desired end? Demonstrate step-by-step how it works. How easy are you making it for them to know, like, and trust you?

Sales is a learning curve, for sure, and the best way I've found to get over it is to get solid on your MESSage. It's a lot easier to offer someone a product or service when you can explain it simply.

And to help you do that, just think ... **O.T.H.E.R.S.**:

Origin – How it came to be.
Testimonials – Who it has already helped.
Help – Understand your process and how it works.

Excited – Show how much you want to help them get
their desired result.
Relief – Remove the stress of working with you/
getting your products.
Solve – Offer the way out of their problem/pain.

Told ya I *love* acronyms! How can you eliminate any confusion a prospect may have about your service/product/offer? Identify and address it!

DON'T CONFUSE OR YOU'LL LOSE

Who is my product/service for?

Who is my product/service *not* for?

What are the typical results/reactions from people
who use my product or service?

What's my guarantee?

How much of *me* do they get with their purchase?

NOTE: *Do this exercise for each of your products/ offers/services.*

PUTTING IT INTO PRACTICE

What would your sales goal have to be in order to achieve____? Examples might include upgrading your computer, sponsoring a missionary, taking a dream vacation, publishing your book— what's your bigger goal/vision/dream?

Now take a look at your calendar and mark how many paydays you need and how much each needs to be in order to reach that goal. This is a powerful motivator! (I mark any of my sales goals in green. Green means go, is a symbol of growth, and the color of the currency that can propel me closer to my dreams.)

Here's a peek at my business, which includes tangible products, digital courses, and in-person/virtual services. I can break each one into different sales goals as well as time frames.

 For example, August, December, and January are peak sales times for the 30-Day Prioritized Focus Success Planner. So promo months for this product are July (back-to-school routine), November (Christmas), and December (New Year's goals).

My live speaking events typically take place between March and April and I offer group coaching from September to November. Each of these has a sales goal, a promotion period with bonuses, launch start/end dates, and a delivery time frame. Do they always go smoothly or as planned? No, but without some type of framework, expectation, and goal in place, how would I even know if I was growing revenue, gaining visibility, or just gushing expenses?

PRACTICE YOUR POTENTIAL PROMOS, PAY DAYS, & PARTNERSHIPS

What's your SALES goal?

By when do you want to achieve this? (this month, quarter, year?)

What products/services will you use to reach the financial goal?

Determine your promotion period (usually 10 days before the "open"/launch):

What do you need to put in place now?

If the idea of sales scares you, either you have not defined your MESSage clearly, you don't believe in your product/offer enough, or you just aren't ready for this gig yet.

Sure, there's a lot more to sales than this, but my goal with this chapter, and the book as a whole, is to get you to take immediate action. I can't—and shouldn't—be your only resource for your forward progress. I'm just a piece of your puzzle, extending my hand if you need a middle-VAL right now.

There you have it. I could go on and on, but I want you to:

Follow-through with your "old business,"
Onboard/Outreach with your "new business,"
Create compelling content to attract new and keep old clients,
Update your lists and communication methods, and
Sell your products/services!

Do you know what the nemesis and enemy of faith, life, and business F.O.C.U.S. is for all of us? Distractions and setbacks. If you're not careful, you can lose your focus and momentum that you worked so hard to *define, discover, and determine* in the previous chapters!

Of course, I'd be remiss if I just left you here. So before we reach the end of our journey together through this book, I have one more important MESSage to share with you.

DO IT!

WE ARE ALMOST FINISHED VAL! Can you believe how far we've come? You've navigated your way through those first 3 Parts, and now we are in the final and probably most challenging section.

But don't worry; it's super short—just one chapter. And remember when I told you in the very beginning that I originally thought this was going to be some type of women's devotional based on a particular biblical passage?

Well, here we are. This final chapter is what I thought the entire book was going to be about. Talk about a full-circle moment!

While I'm kind of sad we're coming to the end of our time together in this book, I'm excited about what's in store for you next.

Let's see what the wilderness has to do with our mess, shall we?

IF YOU TRULY
WANT TO MEASURE
THE SUCCESS OF A
MAN, YOU DO NOT
MEASURE IT BY
THE POSITION HE
HAS ACHIEVED, BUT
BY THE OBSTACLES
HE HAS OVERCOME.

– Booker T. Washington

CHAPTER 13

From WilderMESS to MESSterpiece

SETBACKS, COMEBACKS, & FALLBACKS

EVERY SETBACK CAN BECOME AN EPIC COMEBACK. We know this, hear it, and even applaud the testimonies of those who have lived them. But what about us? Do we have what it takes to overcome our fallback habits and setback mindsets to create testimonies of our own epic comebacks?

When it comes to pursuing our dream, we all have a wilderness to navigate. You know—that dry, desolate, and often lonely place we find ourselves in while on the way to our desired outcome. How long we continue to wander, wonder, and whine in that wilderness depends on us.

Throughout this book, you and I have covered a lot of ground and, prayerfully, overcome many limiting mindsets. Yet despite all of the success we've experienced so far, there is still one area that we have to address: our own wilderness (or as I like to call it, our wilderMESS).

Together in this chapter, we're going to define the difference between a divine wilderness and a self-inflicted wilderMESS, why you land there, discover what it takes to interrupt the pattern, and determine what to do about it!

Handling disappointment, discouragement, and delays on the way to your dream is what this final chapter is all about. And I believe I've found the perfect example to share with you.

VAL, I pray that by this point you are finally beginning to see and own the Valued, Amazing Lady you truly are and how much you are *loved!*

GETTING OUT OF A WILDER*MESS*

Doubt is like quicksand to your forward progress. That's why starting with a solid foundation is so important when it comes to getting out of a wilderness season. For me, that foundation comes from my faith: I either believe God, or I don't. It's that simple *and* that hard.

I believe that God doesn't make mistakes. We sure do though, don't we? Knowing this, it's important to understand that there's a big difference between a wilderness season that we find ourselves in and a wilderMESS season we've created.

The cool thing is that whatever mistakes we make, missteps we take, or mishaps we cause, God isn't gasping in shock. He's not crossing His arms and tapping His foot at us. No, He's waiting to turn all that mess into a beautiful MESSterpiece!

IF ONLY WE WOULD
LOOK UP FROM OUR
WILDER*MESS*, OF
WANDERING IN EVERY
DIRECTION AND
WONDERING WHAT'S
NEXT, WE WOULD
DISCOVER THAT GOD IS
ABLE TO TRANSFORM
OUR WHINING
INTO WINNING.
HE'S WAITING TO
REDIRECT US FROM
OUR WILDERNESS TO
OUR PERSONALIZED
PROMISED LANDS!

Back in Chapter 10, I said that Deuteronomy is one of my go-to places to find encouragement, especially when it comes to God's love and the lengths He'll go to for His people. In particular, Deuteronomy 8 is a brilliant picture of God's ability to not only get us out of our wilderMESS, but also how much He wants us to thrive in our own promised land.

In case you're not too familiar with the Bible story of the Israelites wandering in the desert (aka wilderness) for forty years with Moses as their leader on their way to the land God had promised them (aka the Promised Land), allow me the liberty to share the following with you.

Below you will find *all* of Deuteronomy Chapter 8 along with my personal notes, *exactly* as I originally wrote them next to the corresponding passages in my Bible. My hope is that the Scripture (in italics) and notes together will help express the magnitude of God's provision, protection, and for sure, His promise to us!

DEUTERONOMY 8 (NIV): DO NOT FORGET THE LORD

1 Be careful to follow every command I am giving you today, so that you may live and increase and may enter and possess the land the LORD promised on oath to your ancestors.

MY NOTES:

- the reward → live *and* increase *and* enter *and* possess the land
- how to achieve it → follow every command
- why you can be confident → the Lord promised on oath to your ancestors

*2 Remember how the LORD your God led you all
the way in the wilderness these forty years, to humble
and test you in order to know what was in your heart,
whether or not you would keep his commands.*

MY NOTES:

- What is your wilderness right now? Where is God
  taking you to humble you and get you to *trust* Him?

*3 He humbled you, causing you to hunger and then
feeding you with manna, which neither you nor your
ancestors had known, to teach you that man does not
live on bread alone but on every word that comes from
the mouth of the LORD.*

MY NOTES:

- In the midst of the journey, He not only knows what
  you need, but provides it. Not just provides, but in
  ways you've never seen or known before in order to
  solidify your trust in Him.

*4 Your clothes did not wear out and your feet did not
swell during these forty years.*

MY NOTES:

- Interesting that this is pointed out because in other
  accounts of the Israelites' plight, we learn about how
  much they complained. And not just complained,
  but wanted to go back to slavery in Egypt! So their
  complaining was a mindset issue, not a physical one.

Why would Moses feel the need to point it out? They should have had physical discomfort, but again, God took care of it.

5 Know then in your heart that as a man disciplines his son, so the LORD your God disciplines you.

MY NOTES:

Love. A parent's discipline is because of the *love* they have for their child. To protect, instruct, guide, and for the long-term benefit of the child. We are no different as God's children.

6 Observe the commands of the LORD your God, walking in obedience to him and revering him.

MY NOTES:

We want drive-thru breakthroughs, but observing, walking, and revering are all *present* tense. Meaning, this is an ongoing journey.

7 For the LORD your God is bringing you into a good land—a land with brooks, streams, and deep springs gushing out into the valleys and hills;

MY NOTES:

Trust that "the land" God is bringing you to is *good*, but notice it still has valleys (low) and hills (high). In the midst of the highs and lows, the land God brings us to is still good.

8 a land with wheat and barley, vines and fig trees, pomegranates, olive oil and honey;

MY NOTES:

- Look at the variety of fruits! We were meant to be fruitful, but remember that God can grow and bring many kinds. We aren't meant to bear just *one*.

9 a land where bread will not be scarce and you will lack nothing; a land where the rocks are iron and you can dig copper out of the hills.

MY NOTES:

- Not only will your needs be met, but you will lack *nothing*. That's a *big* promise and it goes even further: "the rocks are iron and you can dig copper" points to profitable work. These were valuable commodities of the day; don't miss what is available once you *get* to your promised land.

10 When you have eaten and are satisfied, praise the LORD your God for the good land he has given you.

MY NOTES:

- What a reminder to be grateful, especially when you are sitting there "fat & happy!"

*11 Be careful that you do not forget the LORD your
God, failing to observe his commands, his laws and his
decrees that I am giving you this day.*

MY NOTES:

* In the middle of this reminder chapter, there's an
urgency to keep the Lord your God the priority.
Failing to observe his commands, laws, and decrees
will be the chief cause of forgetting.

*12 Otherwise, when you eat and are satisfied, when you
build fine houses and settle down, 13 and when your
herds and flocks grow large and your silver and gold
increase and all you have is multiplied,*

MY NOTES:

* Another reminder of *all* that has been provided and
all the ways you have benefitted. In other words,
once you are deemed successful ….

*14 then your heart will become proud and you will
forget the LORD your God, who brought you out of
Egypt, out of the land of slavery. 15 He led you through
the vast and dreadful wilderness, that thirsty and
waterless land, with its venomous snakes and scorpions.
He brought you water out of hard rock. 16 He gave
you manna to eat in the wilderness, something your
ancestors had never known, to humble and test you so
that in the end it might go well with you.*

MY NOTES:

° If you allow your success to get in the way of your focus on God and *all* that He provided, the miraculous ways in which you came by those provisions, and why, your heart will become proud. (God will always take you where you would never go otherwise in order to get you where you need to be and to become who you were meant to be.)

17 You may say to yourself, "My power and the strength of my hands have produced this wealth for me."

MY NOTES:

° If success is the measure and the focus, be careful who gets the credit.

18 But remember the LORD your God, for it is he who gives you the ability to produce wealth, and so confirms his covenant, which he swore to your ancestors, as it is today.

MY NOTES:

° Who gives you the *ability* to produce wealth (success)? God does it for you and has been doing it your whole genealogy. *As entrepreneurs we have to remember that each idea we use is a way of giving back to God. He rewards us with new ideas!

19 If you ever forget the LORD your God and follow other gods and worship and bow down to them, I testify against you today that you will surely be destroyed.

MY NOTES:

- The guarantee that comes with forgetting God, having idols that get more credit and attention than God in our lives.

20 Like the nations the LORD destroyed before you, so you will be destroyed for not obeying the LORD your God.

MY NOTES:

- No one is immune from the consequences; just look at history.

SUMMARY

The wilderness is where God takes us to strengthen us and solidify our identity in Him so that we are prepared for the *good* future He has planned for us—our promised land.

Our wilderMESS is the place between our deliverance from bondage and our promised land. For the Israelites, bondage was literally being slaves to the Egyptians. For us, we have to ask, "What's my Egypt?"

Your "Egypt" is the very thing that prevents you from moving. It might be fear, following someone/something other than God, possessions, pursuits … what is that thing in your life right now?

Know that it's your obedience that determines the speed at which you get to your God-given promised land. Oh, I didn't even get into all that a promised land requires! That might be for another book, but to satisfy the "I need to know" in you right now, I'll summarize by saying it takes belief, battles, and obedience.

MAKING IT STICK

Here is a way to remember how to effectively navigate out of your wandering, wondering, and whining wilderMESS.

YOU HAVE A PROBLEM: WILDER*MESS*

WILD → This is not what I thought my life would be.
"ER" → which way do I go??
MESS → My situation that I just can't seem to get out of!

HE HAS THE SOLUTION: WILDERNESS

WIL → God's plan for you; His will. Trust Him.
"DER" → As in, duh! His Word provides the instructions you need.
NESS → God will use whatever means necessary to show you the way and to remind you that He *loves you*!

Now you know that no matter whether you find yourself in a self-inflicted wilderMESS or a God-ordained wilderness, He's got you! But I still have some practical ways to help you in the midst of it all.

FROM SETBACKS TO COMEBACKS

Of all the things I've learned, gathered, and experienced over the years, I've discovered that time and time again, the following three things help me trade a setback for a comeback:

1. FIND A VERSE, QUOTE, OR MANTRA.

First, find yourself that inspiration! You can't possibly become motivated without first being inspired! What is your go-to quote, verse, or mantra? It's got to be something that sparks the flame in you. You can choose one for each goal you're working on or it can be "the one" that represents your overall God-given dream and mission. The bottom line is it has to deliver; otherwise, you'll stay slumped in setback mode.

2. CHOOSE A FIGHT SONG.

Next, choose a song. I like to call it a fight song because it should garner the same effect as the *Rocky* theme song. If you don't know what I'm talking about, look it up and give it a listen. The song you choose should put you in the mood to fight past the fatigue, pick yourself back up, and keep going!

3. SELECT A TANGIBLE OBJECT.

Finally, you should have something that you can see and touch that also offers an emotional connection. It could be a picture (of your family, your someday dream vacation, house, or car), or a brochure from a charity or organization you want to be able to greatly impact or help. Or it might be an object. Mine for the last several years has been a Lego˚ Minifigure of Wonder Woman right next to my work computer. Yes, I said work computer. If I want to scroll social media or do anything non-work-related, I use my Microsoft˚ Surface tablet or my phone. When it comes to my desktop, that's where my writing gets done and things related to paid income. My little Wonder Woman standing next to my computer reminds me why I'm there. When I feel overwhelmed, she reminds me that I have the power to get over those feelings and keep going.

Now, any one of these is a great help in pulling you out of setbacks and setting you up for a comeback, but when you combine them, you ooze productivity! If that's not the result, go back and reselect motivational reminders until it is. *It's important to remember that motivation is an outward result of an inward inspiration, so if you're not motivated, dig into what truly inspires you!*

TAKE ACTION

Create your comeback inspiration to the point of motivation!

SKIP THE FALLBACKS

You've come a long way, my friend, and I thank you for making it to the end of this book. I am so proud of the work that you've done to get here!

Can I leave you with one last reminder? No matter what life throws at you or who others say that you are, will you promise to remember what we covered together here in this book?

You are **V**alued.
You are **A**mazing.
You are a **L**ady who means business, not just a woman who has a business.

VAL, don't allow your old fallback places, people, and habits to derail you from the journey you are on with God to your promised land.

You are a beautiful MESSterpiece armed with the strategies to answer your God-sized calling with prioritized focus! Now all that's left for you to do is to DO IT!

WHAT'S NEXT?

If you found this book helpful, please consider leaving a review. Your review can help others discover this book and benefit from the information too. Your support is greatly appreciated!

NEED HELPFUL REMINDERS AND ADDITIONAL RESOURCES? I'VE PUT SOME TOGETHER FOR YOU!

Go to
BEAUTIFULMESSTERPIECE.COM
to find them.

CONCLUSION

YOU DID IT, VAL! Picture me over here doing one big happy dance for ya! For real. And if I had your address, you'd be getting one of my favorite "Woo! Hoo!" postcards in the mail, too. :)

While as exciting as it is to accomplish something (in our case, finishing this book together), it's important to apply the lessons you've learned. After all, that was the goal of this book—to be a guide for you to become who you need to be in order to handle the God-given dream that's been entrusted to you.

You've worked your way through the hard yet rewarding inner work of being able to DEFINE who you are beyond your roles, titles, labels, or history. While identifying your core values and why they are so valuable.

I hope you've been able to DISCOVER just where the gaps are in your goal-getting, the myths you fall for, the importance of having the right priorities and peeps in your life, and how to consistently grow in your faith, life, and business. Through Prioritized Focus of course!

Prayerfully, you're DETERMINED to shift your perspective of the messes that have found their way to you, understand the work to get out of them (and limit them in the future), and recognize that they can never mess up Whose you are or what's ultimately been prepared and planned ahead *for you*.

Girl, you even have a comeback plan for when the setbacks occur and you're tempted to rely on those old fallbacks.

Now all you have to do is take those perspectives, truths, tactics, strategies, and resources and **DO IT**! I urge you to pray, plan, and proceed straight toward your God-given dream.

Remember, no mess can hinder you from the progress you were meant to make as His beautiful masterpiece!

Over here cheering you on and praying you up,

ACKNOWLEDGMENTS

NAN & POP, no one saw people as God's workmanship (and MESSterpieces) as clearly as you did. I'm so thankful for your example of agape love that you so effortlessly expressed while you were with us. You are so missed!

MOM & DAD, no one knows the history of my messes, mistakes, and mishaps more than you! Thank you for always encouraging, supporting, and loving me through every single one. God blessed me big-time by giving me you as parents! I hope you know just how loved and appreciated you are.

TO MY HUSBAND, no one has loved this MESSterpiece and supported her crazy ideas and ventures more than you. You're the piece of me that God knew I needed and after all these years, I still feel you're more than I deserve. I love you more than I could ever express. And there's definitely not enough thanks!

TO MY CHILDREN, I pray that you come to know how incredibly brilliant and talented I think you are and how much I have learned from each of you. I love you, am praying for your God-given dreams, and can't wait to see them unfold!

To all of the friends, family, colleagues, prayer warriors, and peeps who have supported this effort—**THANK YOU!**

ABOUT THE AUTHOR

DEANA'S A SASSY, fiercely ambitious, first-time author on a mission to arm Christian women in business to confidently step into their God-given dream.

She's been inspiring women as a solopreneur for nearly a decade. Deana brings practical insights and wisdom to help entrepreneurs and small business owners overcome obstacles and achieve their goals. As a dynamic and engaging speaker, Deana specializes in workshop presentations that equip audiences with the skills and knowledge they need to succeed.

She lives near the Jersey Shore (no, not that one; much further south) and enjoys the crazy conversations and adventures with her family and closest friends.

You can connect with Deana at

DEANAFARRELL.COM